Hebrews and
James

Westminster Bible Companion

Series Editors

Patrick D. Miller
David L. Bartlett

Hebrews and James

FRANCES TAYLOR GENCH

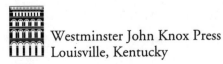
Westminster John Knox Press
Louisville, Kentucky

© 1996 Frances Taylor Gench

Portions of this book originally appeared in the 1992–1993 Horizons Bible Study, *James and the Integrity of Faith* (produced by Horizons for Presbyterian Women, Presbyterian Church [U.S.A.], Louisville, Kentucky, 1992), and are used by permission.

Book design by Publishers' WorkGroup
Cover design by Drew Stevens

First edition

Published by Westminster John Knox Press
Louisville, Kentucky

This book is printed on acid-free paper that meets the American National Standards Institute Z39.48 standard. ∞

PRINTED IN THE UNITED STATES OF AMERICA

96 97 98 99 00 01 02 03 04 05 — 10 9 8 7 6 5 4 3 2 1

Library of Congress Cataloging-in-Publication Data

Gench, Frances Taylor, date.
    Hebrews and James / Frances Taylor Gench.
       p.   cm. — (Westminster Bible Companion)
    Includes bibliographical references.
    ISBN 0-664-25527-2 (alk. paper)
    1. Bible N.T. Hebrews—Commentaries.   2. Bible. N.T. James—Commentaries.   3. Bible. N.T. James. English. New Revised Standard. 1996.   I. Bible. N.T. Hebrews. English. New Revised Standard. 1996. II. Title. III. Series.
BS2725.3.G46   1996
227'87077—dc20   96-21404

Contents

Series Foreword

This series of study guides to the Bible is offered to the church and more specifically to the laity. In daily devotions, in church school classes, and in listening to the preached word, individual Christians turn to the Bible for a sustaining word, a challenging word, and a sense of direction. The word that scripture brings may be highly personal as one deals with the demands and surprises, the joys and sorrows, of daily life. It also may have broader dimensions as people wrestle with moral and theological issues that involve us all. In every congregation and denomination, controversies arise that send ministry and laity alike back to the Word of God to find direction for dealing with difficult matters that confront us.

A significant number of lay women and men in the church also find themselves called to the service of teaching. Most of the time they will be teaching the Bible. In many churches, the primary sustained attention to the Bible and the discovery of its riches for our lives have come from the ongoing teaching of the Bible by persons who have not engaged in formal theological education. They have been willing, and often eager, to study the Bible in order to help others drink from its living water.

This volume is part of a series of books, the Westminster Bible Companion, intended to help the laity of the church read the Bible more clearly and intelligently. Whether such reading is for personal direction or for the teaching of others, the reader cannot avoid the difficulties of trying to understand these words from long ago. The scriptures are clear and clearly available to everyone as they call us to faith in the God who is revealed in Jesus Christ and as they offer to every human being the word of salvation. No companion volumes are necessary in order to hear such words truly. Yet every reader of scripture who pauses to ponder and think further about any text has questions that are not immediately answerable simply by reading the text of scripture. Such questions may be about historical and geographical details or about words that are obscure or so loaded with meaning that one cannot tell at a glance what is at stake. They may be about the fundamental meaning of a passage or about what connection a particular text might have to our contemporary world. Or a teacher preparing for a church school class may simply want to know: What should I say about this biblical passage when I have to teach it next Sunday? It is our hope that these volumes, written by teachers and pastors with long experience studying and teaching the Bible in the church, will help members of the church who want and need to study the Bible with their questions.

The New Revised Standard Version of the Bible is the basis for the interpretive comments that each author provides. The NRSV text is presented at the beginning of the discussion so that the reader may have at hand in a single volume both the scripture passage and the exposition of its meaning. In some instances, where inclusion of the entire passage is not necessary for understanding either the text or the interpreter's discussion, the presentation of the NRSV text may be abbreviated. Usually, the whole of the biblical text is given.

We hope this series will serve the community of faith, opening the Word of God to all the people, so that they may be sustained and guided by it.

Hebrews

Introduction

The Letter to the Hebrews is usually neglected by churchgoers and preachers. This is unfortunate, but the reasons for it are obvious: The language and style of Hebrews are the most erudite in the New Testament, its densely woven argument is complex and sustained, and its imagery of priesthood and sacrificial ritual emerges from an ancient world of thought that is quite foreign to our own.

THE PURPOSE AND THEMES
OF HEBREWS

Yet this book, while not the easiest in the New Testament to comprehend, is among the more unique and valuable treasures of the New Testament. Indeed, those who wrestle with it will find in Hebrews a powerful presentation of the Christian message. Moreover, that message, though addressed to an ancient situation, turns out to be strikingly contemporary in its relevance to our situation today. In sum, Hebrews addresses believers who have grown weary in the Christian way and who are in danger of abandoning their Christian vocation. This can be surmised from clues provided in the letter, noted by my italics:

> We must pay greater attention to what we have heard, *so that we do not drift away from it.* . . . how can we escape *if we neglect so great a salvation?* (2:1–3)

> Take care, brothers and sisters, that none of you may have an evil, unbelieving heart that *turns away* from the living God. (3:12)

> Therefore let us go on toward perfection. . . . For it is impossible to restore again to repentance those who have been enlightened, and have tasted the heavenly gift, and have shared in the Holy Spirit, and have tasted the good-

ness of the word of God and the powers of the age to come, and then have *fallen away*. . . . (6:1–6)

. . . we want each one of you to show the same diligence so as to realize the full assurance of hope to the very end, so that you may not become *sluggish*, but imitators of those who through faith and patience inherit the promises. (6:11–12)

Let us hold fast to the confession of our hope without wavering, for he who has promised is faithful. And let us consider how to provoke one another to love and good deeds, *not neglecting to meet together*, *as is the habit of some*, but encouraging one another, and all the more as you see the Day approaching. (10:23–25)

Therefore *lift your drooping hands* and *strengthen your weak knees*. . . . (12:12)

It is apparent from these clues that Hebrews is addressed to people who have been Christians for some time but who find that their earlier enthusiasm has faded and that their faith commitment has waned. They have grown "sluggish," and are in danger of "drifting" and "falling away." Many have stopped attending the Christian assembly altogether. Moreover, they have ceased to grow in their understanding of the Christian faith (italics added):

About this we have much to say that is hard to explain, since you have become *dull in understanding*. *For though by this time you ought to be teachers, you need someone to teach you again the basic elements of the oracles of God. You need milk, not solid food;* for everyone who lives on milk, being still an infant, is unskilled in the word of righteousness. But solid food is for the mature. . . . (5:11–14)

Clearly, they are in a state of arrested development as Christians! One would not have expected this to be the case, because their earlier history was exemplary. Indeed, they had willingly endured public abuse, even "the plundering of their possessions" for their Christian confession, all the while supporting their fellow Christians in the midst of suffering (italics added):

But recall those earlier days when, after you had been enlightened, you endured a hard struggle with sufferings, sometimes being publicly exposed to abuse and persecution, and sometimes being partners with those so treated. For you had compassion for those who were in prison, and you cheerfully accepted the plundering of your possessions, knowing that you yourselves possessed something better and more lasting. *Do not, therefore, abandon that confidence of yours;* it brings a great reward. For you need *endurance,* so that when you have done the will of God, you may receive what was promised. (10:32–36)

New threats of persecution on the horizon (see 12:3–13; 13:13–14) may have given rise to the community's weariness and discouragement and to the temptation to "drift away" from Christian faith. Whatever may have occasioned the people's lethargy, Hebrews clearly addresses fatigued and beleaguered Christians who suffer from what has aptly been described as "tired blood" (Johnsson, *Hebrews,* 3). They have grown weary in the Christian way and are on the verge of abandoning Christian faith.

Are not these realities remarkably like our own? To this day, Christian communities struggle at times with fading enthusiasm, waning commitment, dwindling church attendance, and arrested development in the Christian faith. In many parts of the world, Christian communities also struggle to keep the faith when faced with opposition and pressure from their circumstances. Hebrews thus continues to address a powerfully relevant word to weary and beleaguered believers who find themselves in danger of "drifting" and losing their Christian vocation. Hebrews speaks a word of grace to all who find themselves in need of encouragement and renewed commitment to the faith.

And what does the author of Hebrews prescribe for this malady? Although the people, in their state of arrested development as Christians, seem ready only for "milk," what they get is "solid food" — a heavy dose of theological reflection! People in this condition need much more than a pep talk. They need a deepened understanding of the person and work of Jesus Christ—the one through whom God has spoken a sure and incomparable word, and through whom are available rich resources for the life of faith. Moreover, Hebrews goes beyond "the basic teaching about Christ" (6:1) to instruct its readers with a creative reinterpretation of the traditions about Jesus. By means of innovative, intellectually challenging solid food indeed, Hebrews aims to rekindle the people's vision, for if they can catch a glimpse of what God has accomplished and made available in him, there would be no thought of drifting from the faith.

The major purpose of Hebrews is thus to encourage, strengthen, and motivate its readers—to call them to faithfulness. The author seeks to achieve this purpose by means of two central themes: priesthood and pilgrimage. First, Hebrews sets forth a new presentation of Jesus as high priest and enthroned Son, through whom faithful Christians have direct access to God. Hebrews is the only book in the New Testament that explores the significance of Jesus' work by means of the priestly image. Like the priests of old, Jesus is a mediator between the human and divine realms, a boundary crosser who opens access to the holy. He cleanses our conscience, removes our sin, and intercedes for us before the throne of grace. His completed work as high priest brings us into the very presence of God and makes possible our own lives of covenant faithfulness.

Second, the theme of pilgrimage is also central, for in his priestly, boundary-crossing role, Jesus is also a trailblazer who leads us to faith's destination, drawing us toward our home with God. Thus Christians are urged to look "to Jesus the pioneer and perfecter of our faith" (12:2) and "to run with perseverance the race that is set before" them (12:1). Hebrews envisions Christian life as a journey, in which we follow Christ's example of faithful service and live as he did, even in the midst of persecution. Christians are to be a pilgrim people, on the move, and sojourners in this world, who seek their home in the city "whose architect and builder is God" (11:10). Thus Hebrews urges its readers to "get the lead out," to keep moving, to get on with their marching toward the goal. The author is anxious to ensure that his weary pilgrims reach the Promised Land. By rekindling their vision of what God has accomplished in Jesus Christ, and by reminding them of the great personal resources available to them through Jesus' completed work, the author of Hebrews seeks to rejuvenate weary readers of every age for the pilgrimage of faith.

THE SERMON FORM OF HEBREWS

Two further observations into the character of Hebrews will help readers understand it. First, note that Hebrews takes the form of a sermon rather than a letter. It does not begin, as do most of the New Testament letters, with an identification of its author and a greeting for its intended readers. Neither the author nor the readers are identified in the opening lines. Instead, Hebrews begins with an impressive christological prologue (that is, a prologue that interprets the significance of Jesus Christ) in 1:1–4. From the way it begins, one might get the impression that Hebrews will take the form of a theological treatise. And to be sure, it presents weighty theological reflection. However, its challenging reflection is by no means abstract. It is geared to a very specific situation—that described above—and conveys a clear pastoral orientation. This is apparent in the author's own designation of his work in 13:22 as a "word of exhortation." Thus Hebrews' theological insights are not presented for their own sake but rather for the purpose of exhorting and encouraging readers.

That Hebrews' "word of exhortation" is sermonic in form is indicated by the fact that it alternates between exposition and application. First the author expounds on the significance of Christ, usually on the basis of a biblical text. Then he applies his christological insights to the life situation of his audience by means of a practical exhortation. This is the kind of speech we recognize on Sunday mornings as a sermon! Biblical commentator William Johnsson (*Hebrews*, 2) helps us see this pattern, which is repeated throughout Hebrews:

Exposition   1:1–14
Exhortation   2:1–4
Exposition   2:5–3:6a
Exhortation   3:6b–4:16
Exposition   5:1–10
Exhortation   5:11–6:20
Exposition   7:1–10:18
Exhortation   10:19–13:25

Thus, in studying Hebrews, one should pay close attention to the alternation between theological exposition and sermonic application. One will note that Hebrews' exposition of the significance of Christ stands in service of its exhortation. Like all good sermons, its reflection does not remain on an abstract and theoretical level. Its theological insights are applied concretely to the lives of its readers. Hebrews has a practical aim and a clear pastoral orientation.

To be sure, Hebrews ends like a letter in 13:20–25, with a benediction and concluding greetings. We may surmise that Hebrews' extended sermon has been sent as a letter to a distant congregation. Still, it is best understood as a sermon, for it has the air of speech rather than of writing. Like most effective preachers, the author speaks in the first person plural ("we," italics added).

Now God did not subject the coming world, about which *we are speaking*, to angels. (2:5)

About this we have much *to say* that is hard *to explain*. . . . (5:11)

Even though *we speak* in this way, beloved. . . . (6:9)

Now the main point in what *we are saying* is this. . . . (8:1)

Of these things *we cannot speak* now in detail. (9:5)

The author makes no reference to his work as a letter or to the act of writing. Hebrews most resembles a sermon—a "word of exhortation"—in which Christians have heard, and can still hear, a clear and sure word about the significance of the person and work of Jesus Christ in the lives that they live today.

THE RELATIONSHIP BETWEEN CHRISTIANITY AND JUDAISM IN HEBREWS

A second notable characteristic of Hebrews is its strong emphasis on both the continuity and discontinuity between Judaism and Christianity. This is apparent in its opening line:

> Long ago God spoke to our ancestors in many and various ways by the prophets, but in these last days [God] has spoken to us by a Son. . . . (1:1–2)

Continuity is apparent, for God has spoken with authority in the past, and the events Hebrews describes are to be viewed within the context of the history of God's dealings with Israel. Discontinuity, however, is apparent as well, for that which takes place in Jesus Christ—God's new agent—is decisive and incomparable. Because the relationship between Judaism and Christianity is marked by continuity and discontinuity, we find in Hebrews both a strikingly Jewish ethos as well as a strong insistence on the superiority of Christianity over Judaism.

On the one hand, one is immediately struck by the decidedly Jewish ethos of Hebrews. As we have noted, Hebrews' argument draws heavily on the imagery of priesthood and on presuppositions of Israel's sacrificial system. Indeed, as we will see, the Day of Atonement (Yom Kippur) ceremonies in particular, and the high priest's role in them, provide the central language and imagery by which Hebrews articulates the work of Christ. Moreover, Old Testament scripture plays a prominent role in the argument of Hebrews. There are thirty actual citations of scripture and more than double that number of allusions. The scriptures, from Hebrews' point of view, are not dead, but are the immediately relevant living word of God—a thoroughly Jewish (and Christian) view of scripture. Hebrews also makes use of an imaginative Jewish method of scripture interpretation called midrash, which seeks to demonstrate both the authority and the relevance of a biblical passage for the community in its present situation.

On the other hand, for all its "Jewishness," one is also struck by Hebrews' notable emphasis on the superiority of Christianity to Judaism. Indeed, Hebrews is distinguished by constant comparisons between the two. "Superior" or "better" turns out to be a key word in the argument: Christ as Son is "better" than the angels (1:5–14), than Moses (3:1–6), than Aaron (5:1–10), and the Levitical priests (7:1–28). His sacrifice is "better" than their sacrifices (9:1–14), and the covenant that he inaugurated is "better" than the first (8:7–13; 9:15–22; 12:24). Moreover, Hebrews does not simply celebrate the superiority of Christianity; it also denigrates ancient Israelite religion and practices, declaring them ineffectual. Indeed, Hebrews claims that the covenant between God and Israel has been "abolished" and replaced by the "better" covenant established in the sacrifice of Jesus Christ (see 8:6–7, 13; 10:9).

What are we to make of this emphasis on the continuity and discontinuity between Christianity and Judaism? In particular, what are we to make of the striking and denigrating comparisons? Traditionally, commentators have supposed that Hebrews addresses Jewish Christians who are tempted to abandon Christian faith in order to return to Judaism and the synagogue. Using comparisons and polemic, the author aims to prevent any such retreat by persuading readers of the inherent superiority of Christianity over Judaism.

While there are interpreters who still hold to some version of this thesis, it has increasingly been called into question, for it can be observed that the comparisons and statements of superiority appear in the expository sections of Hebrews rather than in the exhortations. In the exhortations, which get down to practical matters and apply the author's christological insights to realities facing the life of the congregation, there appears to be no differentiation between the two faiths and no effort to dissuade people of the attractions of Judaism.

Whether or not Hebrews seeks to prevent a retreat to Judaism, we may reasonably assume that Hebrews was originally addressed to a Jewish-Christian audience, who would have understood and appreciated the author's use of scripture and Jewish presuppositions. Furthermore, it is important for us to remember that the first Christians were Jews. Hebrews no doubt reflects a period in the early church's life when Christians and Jews had not yet reached a parting of the ways and when Christians were in the midst of a process of self-definition and differentiation. In the midst of such a process, it would have been natural for Christians to claim superiority for their beliefs over the beliefs of their parent faith and chief competitor. Thus, Hebrews' comparisons and claims of superiority are understandable within a first-century context of differentiation and self-definition.

However, we no longer live in such a context. While the author of Hebrews and his audience still found themselves enmeshed in Judaism, presently Christianity and Judaism have gone their separate ways. Thus, many of Hebrews' claims and comparisons present a problem for contemporary Christian interpretation. Claims that Christianity has replaced Judaism and rendered it obsolete are no longer appropriate in our historical context—indeed, such claims are deeply offensive to our Jewish neighbors. Such claims represent "supersessionist" theology, that is, a theology that holds that Christians have "replaced" or "superseded" Israel in the purposes and affections of God.

This kind of theology, which draws heavily from Hebrews, has had an unfortunate use and misuse in the history of Christian interpretation. It has long been employed to denigrate and discredit Judaism, and thus has had a disastrous and tragic effect on the attitudes of many Christians and consequently on the fate of many Jews. Contemporary Christians must therefore exercise sensitivity and caution in their interpretation and appropriation of Hebrews. Certainly we can appreciate and appropriate Hebrews' powerful witness to God's decisive and sure word in Jesus Christ and its profound theology of access without any accompanying denigration of Judaism.

Moreover, it would serve us well to remember that other New Testament writers, such as Paul, present a different view of the relationship between Christianity and Judaism. As Paul notes in Romans, God's covenant with Israel has by no means been rendered obsolete, nor have Christians replaced Israel in the purposes of God. Instead, he speaks of Christians as "wild" olive branches that have been "grafted" onto Israel's "cultivated olive tree" (see Rom. 11:17–24).

Similarly, the prominent theologian Karl Barth affirmed of the people of Israel that we Christians are "guests in their house, . . . new wood grafted onto their old tree." If we bear this in mind, we will interpret Hebrews in ways that are consistent with the gospel of God's gracious love extended to all people in Jesus Christ.

1. Author and Audience

Originally, none of the New Testament documents had names. The church, however, has found it useful to attach descriptive headings. Thus the document to which we refer has been designated as "The Letter of Paul to the Hebrews." As we have seen, the description of Hebrews as a "letter" is open to question—it is probably best understood as a sermon. Let us also examine the questions of authorship and audience raised by this traditional ascription.

IS PAUL THE AUTHOR OF HEBREWS?

Though Paul's name has long been associated with Hebrews, most interpreters consider it highly unlikely that he is its author. Three reasons are usually cited: First, in all of Paul's undisputed letters, he identifies himself by name as the author, and in the course of his discussion makes frequent reference to his personal experience. However, neither Paul's name nor reference to his experience can be found in Hebrews.

Second, it would appear that both the author and his original audience are one generation removed from those who encountered Jesus directly. They are second-generation Christians. In 2:3, for example, the author says:

> How can we escape if we neglect so great a salvation? It was declared at first through the Lord, and it was attested to us by those who heard him. . . .

The author is apparently neither an eyewitness nor an apostle. Those familiar with the letters of Paul, however, know that he insists emphatically that he has seen the risen Lord and that he makes frequent reference to his apostolic status (see Gal. 1:11–16; Rom. 1:1; 1 Cor. 9:1; 15:8–11).

Third, both the style and theological perspective of Hebrews have long been recognized as uncharacteristic of Paul. The style of Hebrews is the most sophisticated in the New Testament and quite dissimilar to Paul's. Most important, the theological differences between Hebrews and Paul's letters are considerable. Hebrews' presentation of Jesus as high priest is unique in the New Testament, and central Pauline emphases (for example, justification by faith, the church as the body of Christ, and the resurrection of Christ) are not found in Hebrews. In addition, Hebrews and Paul present different twists on the meaning of "faith." For these reasons, Hebrews is widely regarded as an anonymous writing.

Interestingly, this is not an entirely modern conclusion! Many of the earliest Christians expressed doubts about Paul's authorship of Hebrews, and on some of the same grounds noted above. Thus, while the Eastern church early on accepted Hebrews as Pauline, the Western church, centered in Rome, rejected Pauline authorship well into the fourth century. Though after that time Hebrews was generally accepted as Pauline, Paul's authorship was again widely questioned at the time of the Protestant Reformation.

The reformer Martin Luther proposed an alternate candidate who has garnered some support: Apollos, who is described in Acts as "an eloquent man, well-versed in the scriptures" (18:24). Moreover, Apollos is said to have "powerfully refuted the Jews in public, showing by the scriptures that the Messiah is Jesus" (Acts 18:28).

Whoever the author may have been, it is clear that he was indeed eloquent, learned in scripture, skilled in Greek rhetoric, and thus highly educated. Moreover, the reference to Timothy in Hebrews 13:23, who was an associate of Paul's (see 1 Cor. 4:17; 2 Cor. 1:1, 19; 1 Thess. 1:1, 3:2, 6; Phil. 1:1; 2:19), suggests that the author may well have been connected with Pauline circles.

But who wrote Hebrews? Many are content to accept the verdict of Origen of Alexandria (185–254 C.E. [Common Era—formerly designated A.D.]), the greatest scriptural scholar of the ancient church: "Only God knows!"

WHO ARE THE "HEBREWS"?

The recipients of the letter, though not identified within the document itself, have traditionally been referred to as "the Hebrews." This designation has no doubt been made on the basis of the document's contents for, as we have already noted, it does seem to presuppose Jewish-Christian readers. Jewish-Christian readers would have been able to appreciate the author's use of scripture and midrash, as well as the language and imagery of Israel's sacrificial system and priesthood.

But where were they located? One might presume that these Hebrews would be Palestinian Jews. However, it is more likely that the recipients were Diaspora Jews, that is, Jews who lived outside Palestine and were scattered among the nations. They clearly spoke Greek, because the author's quotations of scripture are from the Septuagint (or LXX), the Greek translation of the Hebrew scriptures. Both the author and his audience appear to have been nurtured upon the scripture and traditions of Hellenistic Judaism, that is, the form of Judaism that emerged in urban centers throughout the Greek-speaking world.

While we cannot be sure where, specifically, they were located, the traditional and best guess continues to be Rome. Our only geographical clue is found in Hebrews 13:24, where the author closes by saying: "Greet all your leaders and all the saints. Those from Italy send you greetings." It is thought that the author conveys greetings from fellow Italians back to the home congregation. To be sure, this clue is ambiguous.

The first extrabiblical mention of Hebrews is found in the writings of the ancient church leader Clement of Rome, who in the year 95 C.E. quoted Hebrews extensively. Moreover, the persecution that the recipients are said to have endured (see 10:32–34) may well have been the temporary expulsion of Jews (and thus Jewish Christians) from Rome during the reign of the Emperor Claudius in 49 C.E. The persecution referred to is not thought to be the violent and fiery one that occurred under the Emperor Nero in 64 C.E., for the author notes that the Hebrews "have not yet resisted to the point of shedding [their] blood" (12:4).

All these factors suggest that Hebrews is addressed to second-generation Jewish Christians who perhaps were associated with the larger church at Rome. If so, the letter may be dated in the early 60s, after Claudius's expulsion of Jews and Jewish Christians from Rome and their subsequent return, but before Nero's persecution in 64 C.E. This would also place the composition of Hebrews before the year 70 C.E., in which the Jerusalem Temple was destroyed by the Romans, and Israel's sacrificial cult came to an end. Nothing precludes the composition of Hebrews after the destruction of the Temple in 70 C.E., for Hebrews speaks not of the sacrificial rituals of the sanctuary in Jerusalem but rather of the earlier desert tabernacle sanctuary.

Still, some interpreters find it strange that the author of Hebrews

would not have mentioned the destruction of the Temple if it had occurred, given his interest in Israel's sacrificial system. It would have provided an appropriate capstone for his argument. Thus, Hebrews may be
tentatively assigned to the early 60s. At the latest, we can assume that it
was composed during the years between 60 and 95, when quotations from
it appeared in the writings of Clement of Rome. It must be admitted, however, that we are entirely in the realm of speculation. Fortunately, neither
a precise identification of the author and recipients, nor an accurate date
of the writing are required for us to appreciate the message of Hebrews!

2. Placing Things in Perspective: A Cosmic Panorama
Hebrews 1:1–4

1:1 **Long ago God spoke to our ancestors in many and various ways by the prophets,** 2 **but in these last days he has spoken to us by a Son, whom he appointed heir of all things, through whom he also created the worlds.** 3 **He is the reflection of God's glory and the exact imprint of God's very being, and he sustains all things by his powerful word. When he had made purification for sins, he sat down at the right hand of the Majesty on high,** 4 **having become as much superior to angels as the name he has inherited is more excellent than theirs.**

Hebrews, as we have noted, is addressed to weary Christians in need of rekindled vision, renewed perspective. Thus it opens with a majestic, staggering panorama. It lifts the eyes of its readers to a breathtaking, cosmic plane as it surveys God's purpose in the world and the career of the Son through whom God has spoken decisively. Hebrews' four opening verses are among the most polished and profound in the New Testament, and they introduce key themes. Moreover, by stretching the horizon of Christian vision, they lay the groundwork for a deepened and more mature understanding of the person and work of Jesus Christ.

GOD HAS SPOKEN!

Hebrews strives to set things in perspective for its jaded readers, first of all with an affirmation of the God who has spoken. Indeed, God has never been silent: "Long ago God spoke to our ancestors in many and various ways by the prophets . . ." (1:1). The "prophets" refer to all those through whom God has spoken—from Abraham, through Moses, Joshua, David, and the classical prophets, and thus through all the writers of scripture. And as the biblical witness attests, "in many and various ways" (that is, through dreams and visions and signs, in a burning bush, in a pillar of

cloud and fire, through the presence of angels) God has continually addressed the people. Hebrews proclaims that we are not alone in this uni-
verse! The God whom we confess to be our God is no isolated and remote
deity but one who speaks, who is present to be experienced and known,
who has continually reached out to the creation.

But now, claims Hebrews, "in these last days [God] has spoken to us by
a Son" (1:2). These two opening verses sound the note of continuity and
discontinuity that is central to the argument of Hebrews, as I noted earlier. Continuity is apparent, for God has spoken with power and authority in the past, and the events Hebrews describes are to be viewed within
the context of the plan that God has been unfolding throughout the ages.
"But in these last days" sounds the note of discontinuity: God has spoken
climactically, decisively, and finally through a Son. This new agent of
God's speaking marks, in fact, the appearance of the "last days," the beginning of the end, for in him God's purpose for the world comes to
fruition.

What this means is that we live in a new age. The decisive events in
God's plan for the world—the crucifixion and exaltation of Jesus—have
taken place, and God's purpose for the world now moves toward its completion. What this also means is that the God who speaks, who is present
to be experienced and known, is now known completely. The fullness of
God's revelation is available in a Son. Indeed, as Hebrews goes on to explain, "He is the reflection of God's glory and the exact imprint of God's
very being" (1:3). These are staggering affirmations of the Son's unique
and preeminent status: He is one who partakes of, and mirrors, the very
being and glory of God.

Other New Testament witnesses echo this profound confession. Co-
lossians, for example, praises the Son as "the image of the invisible God"
(Col. 1:15), and in the Gospel of John, Jesus declares that "Whoever has
seen me has seen the Father" (John 14:9). The very being and glory of
God have been extended to us and made known to us—decisively, finally,
and fully by a Son!

THE SON'S COSMIC CAREER

The opening verses of Hebrews address the Son's unique work as well as
his unique status. Indeed, they stretch our horizon and set things in perspective with a breathtaking overview of the Son's cosmic career. That career spans universal history, for God's Son stands at both the beginning

and end of God's purpose for the world. He is there at the beginning, as the very agent of creation, through whom God "created the worlds" (1:2).

The Gospel of John echoes this remarkable claim of the Son's "preexistence" and creative agency in its own prologue: "In the beginning was the Word, and the Word was with God, and the Word was God. . . . All things came into being through him, and without him not one thing came into being" (John 1:1–3). With affirmations such as these, early Christians gave expression to their growing conviction of the ultimate significance of God's Son for the life of the world. So central is he to the meaning and purpose of the world and of all human life that he must have been present at its inception, the very agent of its creation. Moreover, his sustaining power continues to uphold and preserve the world: "He sustains all things by his powerful word" (1:3).

For the author of Hebrews, however, it is during the Son's earthly life that he carries out the work that is most central to his mission and God's purposes: his cross and death, which deal decisively with human sin. Although Hebrews alludes but briefly to this preeminent priestly work in its opening lines ("he had made purification for sins"; 1:3), Christ's once-for-all sacrifice for sins is here introduced and will later receive considerable elaboration.

Finally, Hebrews surveys the last stage of the Son's career: His central work complete, he is exalted to the right hand of God, where he "sits down" and now reigns, superior even to God's heavenly angels (1:3–4). Although, curiously, Hebrews alludes but once to Christ's resurrection (see 13:20), one may assume that exaltation encompasses resurrection. As exalted, reigning Lord, he stands at the end of God's purpose for the world. All things began in him, and will return to him, for God appointed him "heir of all things" (1:2). He is indeed the Alpha and the Omega, as The Revelation to John maintains (Rev. 22:13). He is the beginning and end of all that is. He is the eternal, cosmic Lord!

This is very "high" Christology indeed, that is, a portrait of Christ that highlights his divinity and exalted status. Moreover, in order to articulate the Son's preeminent status and work, the author of Hebrews has made use of a variety of resources at his disposal, two of which are particularly noteworthy.

First, it may be observed that Hebrews draws heavily on the imagery of Lady Wisdom, or Sophia—a striking female figure who emerges in Israel's wisdom literature as an expression of God's own being and gracious outreach to humanity, and as a partner in God's creative work (see especially Proverbs 8—9; Job 28; Wisdom of Solomon 6—9; Sirach 1, 6, 24).

Indeed, Hebrews appears to be directly dependent on the description of Lady Wisdom/Sophia, as found for example in Wisdom of Solomon 7:25–26, which describes her as

> a breath of the power of God, and a pure emanation of the glory of the Almighty. . . . For she is a reflection of eternal light, a spotless mirror of the working of God, and an image of [God's] goodness.

A second resource, Psalm 110, supplies the imagery for Christ's exaltation:

> The Lord says to my lord, "Sit at my right hand until I make your enemies your footstool." (Psalm 110:1)

This psalm, which will provide the imagery of Christ's eternal priesthood as well, plays a prominent role in the argument of Hebrews. Through a creative use of resources such as these, Hebrews strives to rearticulate the significance of Jesus Christ and stretch the limited horizon of its readers.

Hebrews' opening prologue—its staggering panorama—continues to stretch the horizon of Christian vision and to set things in perspective for us. It reminds us that our lives are not products of chance but rather are bound up with the life of God in Christ. God is indeed one in whom "we live and move and have our being" (Acts 17:28).

For God in Christ is at the beginning of our time, as the one who precedes us and creates us, as the one who breathes within our nostrils the breath of life; God in Christ is in the midst of our time, sustaining us and addressing us through Christ's powerful word; and God in Christ is at the end of our days—the frontier ahead, toward which we and the whole creation move. God in Christ represents our past, our present, and our future—"our dwelling place in all generations," as the psalmist said (Psalm 90:1).

Moreover, contemplation of Hebrews' panorama will guard against a restricted vision and limited appreciation of the story of Jesus Christ. Thus it is highly appropriate that the church's lectionary holds this passage before us at Christmas, when we contemplate a baby in a manger. Christians who do not attend church regularly, making an appearance only at Christmas and Easter, may envision Christ only in diapers or nailed to a cross! Hebrews, however, encourages a broader perspective. It fills out the big picture, thereby laying the groundwork for a more mature understanding of the one who stands at the beginning and end of God's purposes for the world, and who makes available to us God's own life.

3. So Great a Salvation!
Hebrews 1:5–2:18

One of the extraordinary things about Hebrews is the equal vigor with which it asserts both the divinity and humanity of Jesus. On the one hand, Hebrews' Christology (that is, its portrait of Jesus) is remarkably "high," which is to say that it places a great deal of emphasis on the divinity and exalted status of Jesus. Thus the prologue affirms that he is the expression of the very being and glory of God, the agent of creation, and the goal toward whom all history is moving (1:1–4).

On the other hand, one finds in Hebrews a decidedly "low" Christology as well, which is to say that its portrait of Jesus is also distinguished by a strong emphasis on Jesus' humanity. Indeed, Hebrews' insistence on the humanity of Jesus, and thus his solidarity with us, is almost without parallel elsewhere in the New Testament.

Both assertions are made in connection with reflection on "angels" in the section that follows. The Son, who is of incomparable majesty, is decidedly superior to the angels (1:5–14), but he took on flesh and blood and thus "for a little while was made lower than the angels" (2:5–18). Hebrews urges us to meditate on this deeply profound paradox and thereby come to a renewed appreciation of the great salvation that God has made available through him.

THE SON'S
SUPERIORITY TO ANGELS
Hebrews 1:5–14

1:5 **For to which of the angels did God ever say,**
    "You are my Son;
    today I have begotten you"?
Or again,
    "I will be his Father, and he will be my Son"?

19

[6] And again, when he brings the firstborn into the world, he says,
    "Let all God's angels worship him."
[7] Of the angels he says,
    "He makes his angels winds, and his servants flames of fire."
[8] But of the Son he says,
    "Your throne, O God, is forever and ever,
        and the righteous scepter is the scepter of your kingdom.
    [9] You have loved righteousness and hated wickedness;
    therefore God, your God, has anointed you
        with the oil of gladness beyond your companions."
[10] And,
    "In the beginning, Lord, you founded the earth,
        and the heavens are the work of your hands;
    [11] they will perish, but you remain;
        they will all wear out like clothing;
    [12] like a cloak you will roll them up
        and like clothing they will be changed.
    But you are the same, and your years will never end."
[13] But to which of the angels has he ever said,
    "Sit at my right hand until I make your enemies
    a footstool for your feet"?
[14] Are not all angels spirits in the divine service, sent to serve for the sake of
    those who are to inherit salvation?

Hebrews' prologue in 1:1–4 concluded with an affirmation of the Son's exalted status and enthronement at the right hand of God, noting that he had become "superior to angels" and had inherited a name "more excellent than theirs." Hebrews 1:5–14 continues this line of thought with an extended exposition of the Son's superiority to angels. Seven Old Testament quotations elaborate this claim, all of which are construed as utterances of God to or about the Son.

The first two quotations, in verse 5 (from Psalm 2:7 and 2 Sam. 7:14), confirm that no angel has ever been called "Son." The next two quotations, in verses 6–7 (from Deut. 32:43, as it appears in the Septuagint, and Psalm 104:4), confirm the angels' subordinate role: Indeed, the angels worship the Son and serve God in a position inferior to that of the Son as God's messengers and ministers. The last three quotations, in verses 8–14 (from Psalm 45:6–7; 102:25–27; 110:1), highlight the Son's exalted role and incomparable status: He is without peer, worthy to be addressed as "God"; though all else fades away, he is unchanging and endures forever, and he has been exalted to the right hand of God, where he now reigns until the day when all things are finally subject to him. The angels occupy no such role in the purposes of God. Indeed, they are but "spirits in the divine service" (1:14), ministers of God's saving concern for us.

Though the author's point—the Son's superiority to angels—is unmistakably clear, two aspects of this passage are likely to strike today's readers as exceedingly peculiar: (1) its preoccupation with angels and (2) its use of scripture. The preoccupation with angels may seem odd, for many Christians in our day do not believe in angelic beings—divine messengers. However, there is no denying that in recent years angels have become a source of considerable cultural fascination. Angel books now crowd bestseller lists, and bookstores have had to establish angel sections. Indeed, angel artifacts have become big business, as New Age religions have given rise to angel boutiques, angel catalogs, angel newsletters, angel seminars, and angel sightings. Some observers see the surge of interest in angels as a sign of a spiritual awakening in our culture, while others see it rather as a sign of spiritual confusion. Whatever the case may be, Hebrews addresses a relevant word to Christians, ancient and modern, who encounter angel speculation.

In the first century, angels were also of great interest in both Greek and Jewish religious thinking. Some interpreters speculate that Hebrews addresses Christians who may have been engaged in some sort of angel worship; others speculate that Jewish-Christian readers may have held Jesus to be an angel (rather than an expression of God's own self) in order to avoid compromising monotheistic faith (belief in one God). We cannot know for sure what prompted the author's great interest in this subject. What we do know is that he is eager, for whatever reason, to impress upon his readers the preeminent status and role of the Son in the purposes of God. He brooks no rivals! Angels, though important creatures of God, cannot compare with God's Son.

Hebrews' use of scripture, both in this passage and throughout the work, is also likely to strike contemporary readers as peculiar. Indeed, it would appear that the author plucks passages out of their original context in the Old Testament and misconstrues them in presenting them as divine utterances to or about God's Son. To give but one example, we know that Psalms 2 and 110 (quoted in verses 5 and 13), are "enthronement psalms," which, in their original context, address God's word to ancient Israelite kings upon the occasion of their installation. They are not self-evidently words about Jesus!

This kind of biblical interpretation is likely to strike modern readers as suspect; however, the author employs an ancient and respected method of Jewish scriptural interpretation. Moreover, we should not suppose that

Hebrews seeks to "prove" the superior status of the Son to angels by means of these quotations. Instead the author brings his conviction that Jesus Christ is Lord to his reading of the scriptures, and there finds his conviction "confirmed." In his view, the scriptures, full of promise and anticipation, point toward the fulfillment of God's purposes in Jesus Christ.

A WARNING NOT TO NEGLECT
SO GREAT A SALVATION
Hebrews 2:1–4

> 2:1 **Therefore we must pay greater attention to what we have heard, so that we do not drift away from it.** [2] **For if the message declared through angels was valid, and every transgression or disobedience received a just penalty,** [3] **how can we escape if we neglect so great a salvation? It was declared at first through the Lord, and it was attested to us by those who heard him,** [4] **while God added his testimony by signs and wonders and various miracles, and by gifts of the Holy Spirit, distributed according to his will.**

In Hebrews, theological reflection never remains on an abstract level. The author constantly applies his insights to the life situation of his audience with a practical exhortation. Thus a key word in his argument is "Therefore" (see 2:1; 3:1, 7; 4:1, 11, 16; 6:1; 10:19; 12:1, 12, 28). Christian living is always a "therefore" kind of living. God's demonstration of love for us in Jesus Christ calls for an appropriate response.

Hebrews 2:1–4 is the first of many exhortations and is also our first hint that all is not well with its readers. From the author's perspective, they are in grave danger of "drifting away" from the faith. It is for this reason that he has held before them the lordship and incomparable majesty of God's Son, hoping to rekindle their appreciation of the great gift of salvation that God has made available in him.

Sometimes gifts, however, can be taken for granted. The author finds it unthinkable that God's precious gift should be neglected or taken lightly when it should be prized above all else and shared with others. Thus, with a word of warning, he alludes to the consequences of neglect. He notes that the law delivered at Mount Sinai through the agency of angels (see Acts 7:38, 53; Gal. 3:19) entailed "just penalties" if disobeyed.

How much more so will neglect of the one who is superior to angels incur just punishment: "How can we escape if we neglect so great a salvation?" (2:3). The precious reality of God's gift is attested in four ways: by the Lord himself, by eyewitnesses, by God's own testimony "by signs and wonders and various miracles," and by the Holy Spirit (2:3–4).

This exhortation continues to be relevant, for often it is "drifting" or neglect, rather than outright rejection, that most jeopardizes Christian faith. As commentator Herbert Chilstrom observes,

> To put off devotional reading "until tomorrow," to miss worship "just this one Sunday," to postpone teaching Sunday church school "until next year," to give more generously "once I get a better job"—these are the stuff of neglect. And neglect, more than open rejection, has most often been the reason why people become lost from the church and from the faith. (*Hebrews*, 14–15)

Therefore we, too, "must pay greater attention to what we have heard, so that we do not drift away from it"!

JESUS, "FOR A LITTLE WHILE . . . LOWER THAN THE ANGELS"
Hebrews 2:5–18

2:5 Now God did not subject the coming world, about which we are speaking, to angels. 6 But someone has testified somewhere,
> "What are human beings that you are mindful of them,
>   or mortals, that you care for them?
> 7 You have made them for a little while lower than the angels;
>   you have crowned them with glory and honor,
> 8 subjecting all things under their feet."

Now in subjecting all things to them, God left nothing outside their control. As it is, we do not yet see everything in subjection to them, 9 but we do see Jesus, who for a little while was made lower than the angels, now crowned with glory and honor because of the suffering of death, so that by the grace of God he might taste death for everyone.

10 It was fitting that God, for whom and through whom all things exist, in bringing many children to glory, should make the pioneer of their salvation perfect through sufferings. 11 For the one who sanctifies and those who are sanctified all have one Father. For this reason Jesus is not ashamed to call them brothers and sisters, 12 saying,
> "I will proclaim your name to my brothers and sisters,
>   in the midst of the congregation I will praise you."

13 And again,
> "I will put my trust in him."

And again,

  "Here am I and the children whom God has given me."

[14] Since, therefore, the children share flesh and blood, he himself likewise shared the same things, so that through death he might destroy the one who has the power of death, that is, the devil, [15] and free those who all their lives were held in slavery by the fear of death. [16] For it is clear that he did not come to help angels, but the descendants of Abraham. [17] Therefore he had to become like his brothers and sisters in every respect, so that he might be a merciful and faithful high priest in the service of God, to make a sacrifice of atonement for the sins of the people. [18] Because he himself was tested by what he suffered, he is able to help those who are being tested.

One thing would seem to stand in opposition to the insistence in Hebrews on the exalted status and incomparable majesty of God's Son. How can such divine majesty be true of a human being? How can this be true of one who lived in a remote corner of the Roman Empire, who never traveled more than a hundred miles from home, and who suffered and died a terrible, humiliating death on a cross? Can such a person be said to be the agent of creation and the goal toward whom all things are moving?

The author of Hebrews does not shrink from this paradox. Indeed, the Son's full humanity is held to be essential to God's plan of salvation. Thus in 2:5–18 we find what is perhaps the most profound statement of Jesus' humanity and solidarity with us in the New Testament. Hebrews declares that God's own Son, who is of incomparable majesty and decidedly superior to angels, for a little while was made lower than the angels! He took on flesh and blood and fully shared our human lot. Indeed, "he had to become like his brothers and sisters in every respect" (2:17), for this was "fitting" (2:10)—it was part of God's plan.

How so? What did Jesus' full humanity achieve in the purposes of God? It achieved three things. First, Jesus embodied humanity as it was meant to be and achieved the purpose for which we were created, in that he lived a life of perfect obedience before God. Psalm 8 is quoted in verses 6–8 as a reminder of the wonder and glory of the human creature, to whom God gave dominion over the created order. However, we do not yet see that dominion (2:8). God's wondrous design for humanity was not to be realized. As the sad story of Adam, the first human, attests, it was thwarted by disobedience—by the reality of sin. However, "we do see Jesus" (2:9), whom Hebrews presents as the second or last Adam and true human, who embodies in himself the glory and dominion that the first Adam and his children lost because of sin. As the second or last Adam, Christ restores to the human race the righteousness of life lost by the first Adam (see also Rom. 5:14; 1 Cor. 15:45).

Thus when we look at Jesus we see fully revealed not only who God is, but also who we are meant to be. Though he entered fully into the realm of sin, the arena of human temptation and suffering, and thereby shared the struggle in which we are engaged, in his death he offered a life of perfect obedience and absolute holiness to God. Consequently, he passed through death to a position of glory and honor, and became the "pioneer" of our salvation, the trailblazer, who brings the rest of humanity to the same position (2:10).

Second, Jesus has freed us from the fear of death by sharing our "flesh and blood" (2:14–15). He experienced the full reality of our human condition, in that he suffered death—the final reality that every human creature faces. But "now crowned with glory and honor" in his resurrection (2:9), he gives reassurance to everyone who faces death—which is all of us! Many of us can identify with the comedian who remarked: "It's not that I'm afraid to die. I just don't want to be there when it happens." Neither do we want to be there when it happens, and those moments in which we are grasped by an awareness of our finitude can have paralyzing power.

What Hebrews proclaims, however, is that we no longer need be paralyzed by fear of death. Though we live in the interim period between the decisive cross and resurrection of Jesus and the final fulfillment of God's purposes, and thus still experience death, we know that its power is limited and will come to an end. Christians are not enslaved by the fear of death. With Paul, we are able to affirm: "Death has been swallowed up in victory. Where, O death, is your victory? Where, O death, is your sting?" (1 Cor. 15:55). We know that death is not the last word, for the "pioneer" of our salvation will bring us also into the glorious communion that he shares with God.

Finally, by sharing our flesh and blood, Jesus has complete sympathy and solidarity with our human condition. He knows the struggle in which we are engaged—from the inside! He knows what it is like to be a weak, broken, wounded human being. Indeed, so complete is his identification with us that he is family (see 2:11–17).

Hebrews presents the stunning claim that the exalted Son of God, the agent of creation and the goal toward whom all history moves (1:1–4), "is not ashamed" to call us "brothers and sisters" (2:11). His complete sympathy and solidarity with us as a brother qualifies him ("perfects him") to be our merciful and faithful high priest, for one who would represent us before God must know our struggles and identify with us completely.

Thus, whatever our experience, we can never say that God does not understand. God does! Moreover, we are not without help. Hebrews affirms that "because [Christ] himself was tested by what he suffered, he is able to help those who are being tested" (2:18). He is able to bring God's grace and strength to bear on our human struggles.

At the close of this passage then, Hebrews introduces its great theme: the high priesthood of Jesus Christ. It also notes the two dimensions of this office: sympathetic intercession in our behalf (highlighted in this passage) and sacrifice for atonement of sins (which will receive elaboration in chapters to follow). How great a salvation indeed!

4. A Call to Faithfulness
Hebrews 3:1–4:13

Throughout Hebrews, the author strives repeatedly to focus the thoughts of his readers on Jesus and the significance of his person and work. In 3:1–6, the characteristic of Jesus that the author places in sharpest relief is his faithfulness. This leads, in 3:7–4:13, to an extended exhortation on faithfulness. The lives of believers are to be marked by the same fidelity that distinguished the life of Jesus! The exhortation is a critical one, since it is being addressed to believers who are on the verge of abandoning their Christian vocation—of falling away from the faith.

JESUS AND MOSES: EXAMPLES OF FAITHFULNESS
Hebrews 3:1–6

> 3:1 **Therefore, brothers and sisters, holy partners in a heavenly calling, consider that Jesus, the apostle and high priest of our confession,** 2 **was faithful to the one who appointed him, just as Moses also "was faithful in all God's house."** 3 **Yet Jesus is worthy of more glory than Moses, just as the builder of a house has more honor than the house itself.** 4 **(For every house is built by someone, but the builder of all things is God.)** 5 **Now Moses was faithful in all God's house as a servant, to testify to the things that would be spoken later.** 6 **Christ, however, was faithful over God's house as a son, and we are his house if we hold firm the confidence and the pride that belong to hope.**

Hebrews' designation of Jesus as both "apostle" and "high priest" should give us pause (3:2). Only here in the New Testament is Jesus referred to as an "apostle"—a word that comes from the Greek word *apostellō*, which means "to send out." Apostles are messengers sent to speak God's word. As we have seen, Hebrews does indeed view Jesus as one sent from God,

27

who represents God to humanity (see 1:1–4). At the same time, he is "high priest," in that he also represents humanity to God. We may take comfort and encouragement from the fact that the one who serves in this capacity—who speaks both God's word to us and our word to God—is distinguished by his faithfulness to these tasks! God's apostle and our high priest is one on whom we can rely completely.

In order to underscore the faithfulness of Jesus, Hebrews proceeds with a stunning comparison. Comparison, as we know, plays a major role in the argument of Hebrews, for we have already been apprised of the Son's superiority to angels (see 1:5–14). For his second comparison, however, the author points to Moses, the greatest hero and prophet of ancient Israel. Consider God's faithful servant, Moses—through whom God delivered Israel from bondage in Egypt and gave them the law, who alone among all the prophets spoke face-to-face with God (Num. 12:6–8)—and know that Jesus' faithfulness is even greater! Moses' faithfulness is by no means denigrated; indeed, the comparison derives its impact from the fact that Jesus is superior even to such a one as this.

But while both Moses and Jesus are distinguished by their faithfulness to the purposes of God, Jesus "is worthy of more glory than Moses" (3:3), for though Moses "was faithful *in* all God's house as a *servant*," Christ "was faithful *over* God's house as a *son*" (3:5–6; italics added). The point is that a child of a house (the Son), enjoys a status and direct relationship with the parent (God) that a servant in the house, no matter how faithful, cannot claim. Moreover, while Moses, Israel's greatest prophet, testified "to the things that would be spoken later," the Son *is* God's decisive and final word (1:1–2)—the fulfillment of prophecy. Such a comparison would not fail to make an impact on Jewish-Christian readers. It would serve as a powerful reminder of just how trustworthy and unequalled is their "merciful and faithful high priest" (2:17), who brings their concerns before the throne of God.

At the close of the comparison, Hebrews observes that the lives of believers are to be marked by the same fidelity that distinguished the lives of Moses and Jesus. Indeed, one little word—"if"—serves as a reminder that membership among the people of God ("God's house") is not automatic: "We are [God's] house if we hold firm the confidence and the pride that belong to hope" (3:6; see also 3:14). Thus the author's thoughts turn once again to the life situation of his readers, whom he perceives to be in grave danger of drifting from the faith. These thoughts lead to an extended digression on the urgency of faithfulness.

A HISTORY LESSON
ON FAITHFULNESS
Hebrews 3:7–4:13

3:7 Therefore, as the Holy Spirit says,
>   "Today, if you hear his voice,
> 8   do not harden your hearts as in the rebellion,
>   as on the day of testing in the wilderness,
> 9   where your ancestors put me to the test,
>   though they had seen my works 10 for forty years.
>   Therefore I was angry with that generation,
>   and I said, 'They always go astray in their hearts,
>   and they have not known my ways.'
> 11 As in my anger I swore, 'They will not enter my rest.' "

12 Take care, brothers and sisters, that none of you may have an evil, unbe-
lieving heart that turns away from the living God. 13 But exhort one another
every day, as long as it is called "today," so that none of you may be hardened by the deceitfulness of sin. 14 For we have become partners of Christ,
if only we hold our first confidence firm to the end.
15 As it is said,

>   "Today, if you hear his voice
>   do not harden your hearts as in the rebellion."

16 Now who were they who heard and yet were rebellious? Was it not all
those who left Egypt under the leadership of Moses? 17 But with whom was
he angry forty years? Was it not those who sinned, whose bodies fell in the
wilderness? 18 And to whom did he swear that they would not enter his rest,
if not to those who were disobedient? 19 So we see that they were unable to
enter because of unbelief.

4:1 Therefore, while the promise of entering his rest is still open, let
us take care that none of you should seem to have failed to reach it. 2 For
indeed the good news came to us just as to them; but the message they
heard did not benefit them, because they were not united by faith with
those who listened. 3 For we who have believed enter that rest, just as
God has said,

>   "As in my anger I swore,
>   'They shall not enter my rest,' "

though his works were finished at the foundation of the world. 4 For in one
place it speaks about the seventh day as follows, "And God rested on the
seventh day from all his works." 5 And again in this place it says, "They shall
not enter my rest." 6 Since therefore it remains open for some to enter it,
and those who formerly received the good news failed to enter because of
disobedience, 7 again he sets a certain day—"today"—saying through David
much later, in the words already quoted,

> "Today, if you hear his voice,
> do not harden your hearts."

[8] For if Joshua had given them rest, God would not speak later about another day. [9] So then, a sabbath rest still remains for the people of God; [10] for those who enter God's rest also cease from their labors as God did from his. [11] Let us therefore make every effort to enter that rest, so that no one may fall through such disobedience as theirs.

[12] Indeed, the word of God is living and active, sharper than any two-edged sword, piercing until it divides soul from spirit, joints from marrow; it is able to judge the thoughts and intentions of the heart. [13] And before him no creature is hidden, but all are naked and laid bare to the eyes of the one to whom we must render an account.

If Hebrews is best understood as a sermon, a "word of exhortation" for its readers, it is also apparent that the work as a whole contains a number of minisermons. One such "sermonette" is found in 3:7–4:13 and constitutes a call to faithfulness. Its springboard is a biblical text, Psalm 75, from which emerge three key themes and a compelling sermon illustration.

The first theme is that of faithfulness versus faithlessness, which is explored by means of a negative example: infidelity exhibited by the exodus generation. Those whom Moses led out of Egypt hardened their hearts in rebellion against God during their forty years of desert wandering. Though God delivered them from slavery and provided manna and water in the wilderness, they continually complained and refused to place their trust in God (see Exodus 15—17). Their infidelity and disobedience had dire consequences, for they prevented them from entering into God's "rest" (3:19). Indeed, Psalm 75 serves as a reminder of God's judgment against such rebellion and hardness of heart.

The author of Hebrews hopes that his readers can learn something from this unfortunate history lesson, for he is alarmed to find them in a similar situation—on the verge of the same unbelief that incurred God's judgment. The striking parallels between their situation and that of the exodus generation should bring them to their senses! Like the ancient Israelites, they, too, have experienced a great act of divine deliverance in the cross of Jesus Christ. They, too, have set out on a journey—a pilgrimage of faith. Yet they, too, now find themselves in danger of falling away. Will they, then, also incur God's wrath and judgment and fail to enter God's promised "rest"?

The second key theme of the minisermon, God's promise of rest, is multilayered. Initially, in 3:7–19 in connection with the exodus generation, it refers to rest from enemies in the promised land of Canaan. In

4:1–11, however, the concept is expanded by means of Genesis 2:2, which speaks of the sabbath rest that God entered upon the completion of creation. "Rest" is to be understood, then, essentially as a heavenly reality and spiritual experience. The promise of rest, which the exodus generation failed to embrace, still stands—God's word does not return to God empty. The promise is still extended: Christians are invited to share God's own rest—God's own life. Hebrews, as we have noted, envisions Christian life as a pilgrimage, a journey toward a heavenly city (11:13–16), and rest is an appealing concept to travellers. When do we enter into it?

As biblical scholar Harold Attridge has pointed out, "rest" appears to be a complex symbol for the whole process of salvation. It is "the process of entry into God's presence," a journey that we begin at the moment of our baptism (10:22) and that will be completed on the last day, when God's purposes for the world reach their fulfillment (Attridge, *The Epistle to the Hebrews*, 128). "Rest," therefore, has both present and future dimensions. It is a present reality in our lives when, in the midst of whatever befalls us in our journey of faith, we experience the peace, assurance, and confidence that comes from knowing that our lives are secure in the purposes and promises of God. That sense of security and well-being is also a foretaste of the eternal rest we will one day enjoy in fullness.

Thus, in the passage before us, Hebrews speaks of "rest" in both its present and future senses, on the one hand affirming that "we who have believed enter that rest" (4:3), while on the other hand urging its readers to keep moving toward the goal and to "make every effort to enter that rest" (4:11). It is a complex concept indeed, but an appealing one to Christian pilgrims of every age, who may find themselves buffeted by the realities of their respective journeys but nevertheless at peace and secure in God's promise of rest. Augustine of Hippo, a bishop of the early Christian church, captured the reality of which Hebrews speaks in a memorable prayer: "You have made us for yourself, O God, and our hearts are restless still, until they rest in you."

A final key theme is the daily challenge of Christian life. With the repetition of the word "today," Hebrews underlines the fact that every day of our lives presents opportunities for faithfulness, for responding in obedience to the promises of God. Indeed, faithfulness, as Hebrews speaks of it, is far more than intellectual assent. It involves fidelity and perseverance as we seek to follow in the path that Christ has set before us and to embody God's purposes for human life.

In the midst of this challenging journey, we need the encouragement and support of fellow pilgrims. Thus Hebrews urges its readers not to neglect Christian fellowship (10:25) but rather to "exhort one another every day, . . . so that none of you may be hardened by the deceitfulness of sin" (3:13). We are not alone as we face the daily challenge of the Christian journey, for we travel in the company of fellow pilgrims on a trail that has already been blazed by Jesus, "the pioneer and perfecter of our faith" (2:10; 12:2). Moreover, as our great high priest, he brings God's grace and strength to bear on our pilgrimage. Great resources are available to us as we face the daily challenge of Christian life!

The author of Hebrews concludes his minisermon on faithfulness with a stern warning in 4:12–13. The matter he has been discussing is an urgent one, for he fears that his readers are on the verge of faithlessness, of falling away from the living God. Thus, in closing, he reminds them of the utter seriousness of their decision in this matter: God "is able to judge the thoughts and intentions of the heart. And before [God] no creature is hidden, but all are naked and laid bare to the eyes of the one to whom we must render an account" (4:12–13). May Hebrews' vision of the great salvation that God has made available in Christ rekindle in all of us faithful and responsive hearts!

5. A Call to Maturity
Hebrews 4:14–6:20

In 4:14–6:20, Hebrews begins to set the stage for its central exposition of the high priesthood of Jesus Christ. The author fears, however, that his innovative presentation of the person and work of Christ may be beyond the reach of the sluggish Christians whom he addresses. They have ceased to grow in the Christian faith, and in their present state of arrested development as Christians they may not be able to digest what he has to say. Thus, before proceeding any further, he issues an urgent call to maturity and informs them of his intention to exercise their sluggish minds and hearts with mature teaching.

JESUS, THE SYMPATHETIC HIGH PRIEST
Hebrews 4:14–5:10

4:14 **Since, then, we have a great high priest who has passed through the heavens, Jesus, the Son of God, let us hold fast to our confession. [15] For we do not have a high priest who is unable to sympathize with our weaknesses, but we have one who in every respect has been tested as we are, yet without sin. [16] Let us therefore approach the throne of grace with boldness, so that we may receive mercy and find grace to help in time of need.**

5:1 **Every high priest chosen from among mortals is put in charge of things pertaining to God on their behalf, to offer gifts and sacrifices for sins. [2] He is able to deal gently with the ignorant and wayward, since he himself is subject to weakness; [3] and because of this he must offer sacrifice for his own sins as well as for those of the people. [4] And one does not presume to take this honor, but takes it only when called by God, just as Aaron was.**

[5] **So also Christ did not glorify himself in becoming a high priest, but was appointed by the one who said to him,**

> "You are my Son, today I have begotten you";
> [6] as he says also in another place,
> "You are a priest forever, according to the order of Melchizedek."
> [7] In the days of his flesh, Jesus offered up prayers and supplications, with loud cries and tears, to the one who was able to save him from death, and he was heard because of his reverent submission. [8] Although he was a Son, he learned obedience through what he suffered; [9] and having been made perfect, he became the source of eternal salvation for all who obey him, [10] having been designated by God a high priest according to the order of Melchizedek.

Hebrews opens, in 4:14–16, with a renewed call to faithfulness. They are among the grandest words of assurance in the New Testament, for they remind us that the life of faithfulness does not depend on our own strength, determination, or subjective state. It depends, rather, on an objective reality: "Since, then, we have a great high priest . . . let us hold fast to our confession. . . . Let us therefore approach the throne of grace with boldness. . . "(vv. 14–16). To that external reality we may cling, "despite passing states of feeling or waves of hard times which may wash over us" (Johnsson, *Hebrews*, 34).

Indeed, it is Jesus Christ, our great high priest, who enables Christians to remain faithful. Though he is the exalted Son of God, "who has passed through the heavens" into God's very presence, he is by no means distant from us. He has a unique capacity to "sympathize with our weaknesses," for he has also fully experienced our human condition: "In every respect" he "has been tested as we are." As a result of his human experience, compassion, and present exalted status, he is able to help us! He is able to lead us also into God's presence and to bring God's grace and strength to bear on our struggles in times of need.

Hebrews proceeds, then, to set the stage for its presentation of Jesus as high priest by reviewing the role and qualifications of ordinary human high priests in 5:1–4. The role is that of mediator between humanity and God: "Every high priest chosen from among mortals is put in charge of things pertaining to God on their behalf, to offer gifts and sacrifices for sin" (5:1). Moreover, Hebrews highlights two central qualifications for this role. First, a high priest must be merciful, and in the case of an ordinary human high priest, solidarity with the human condition ensures this, for "he himself is subject to weakness; and because of this he must offer sacrifice for his own sins as well as for those of the people" (5:2–3). The second qualification is divine appointment, for "one does not presume to take this honor, but takes it only when called by God" (5:4).

Hebrews goes on in 5:5–10, then, to note that Jesus is uniquely qualified for his role as high priest on both counts. In the first place, he too is
high priest by divine appointment. The unique aspect of his appointment,
however, emerges from the fact that he is God's own Son (5:5) and has received an eternal priesthood ("You are a priest *forever*, according to the order of Melchizedek"; 5:6)—aspects of his priesthood that will receive considerable elaboration in Hebrews 7—10.

Moreover, he too is merciful and stands in solidarity with humanity—
not, however, because "he himself is subject to weakness" and "must offer
sacrifice for his own sins," for he is without sin (4:15). Jesus is a merciful
high priest, rather, because "although he was a Son," he became fully human and "learned obedience through what he suffered" (5:8). He was
thereby "made perfect," that is, qualified for his office as high priest, for
as a result of his human experience he is able to sympathize with those
whom he represents.

Throughout 4:14–5:10 we see once again the extraordinary dual emphasis on the divinity and exalted status of Jesus, as well as his full humanity. In 5:7 especially, which many take to be a reference to either his
experience at Gethsemane or Golgotha, his humanity is vividly portrayed.
It cannot be overemphasized how integral both Jesus' divine sonship and
his genuine humanity are to Hebrews' presentation of him as our great
high priest. Because he is intimately related to God, he leads us into God's
own presence. Because he is genuinely human, he is sympathetically
linked to us. His priesthood combines both divine sonship and humanity,
and it is this that makes his priesthood truly unique!

A WORD OF WARNING
Hebrews 5:11–6:8

5:11 **About this we have much to say that is hard to explain, since you have
become dull in understanding.** [12] **For though by this time you ought to be
teachers, you need someone to teach you again the basic elements of the oracles of God. You need milk, not solid food;** [13] **for everyone who lives on
milk, being still an infant, is unskilled in the word of righteousness.** [14] **But
solid food is for the mature, for those whose faculties have been trained by
practice to distinguish good from evil.**

6:1 **Therefore let us go on toward perfection, leaving behind the basic
teaching about Christ, and not laying again the foundation: repentance from
dead works and faith toward God,** [2] **instruction about baptism, laying on of
hands, resurrection of the dead, and eternal judgment.** [3] **And we will do this,**

if God permits. ⁴ For it is impossible to restore again to repentance those who have once been enlightened, and have tasted the heavenly gift, and have shared in the Holy Spirit, ⁵ and have tasted the goodness of the word of God and the powers of the age to come, ⁶ and then have fallen away, since on their own they are crucifying again the Son of God and are holding him up to contempt. ⁷ Ground that drinks up the rain falling on it repeatedly, and that produces a crop useful to those to whom it is cultivated, receives a blessing from God. ⁸ But if it produces thorns and thistles, it is worthless and on the verge of being cursed; its end is to be burned over.

The stage has now been set for an extended discussion of the high priest-hood of Jesus Christ. Before proceeding, however, the author turns once again to exhort his readers. He is about to lay upon them some rather weighty theological reflection. He has "much to say that is hard to explain" (5:11) but they have ceased to grow in their Christian faith. They have become "sluggish," "dull in understanding" (5:11; 6:12)—and thus he fears that his message will be beyond their reach. He pauses, therefore, to express his exasperation over their arrested development as Christians. They have, in fact, regressed, for though they have been Christians long enough to have reached the point where they should be able to teach others, they need someone to teach them again the basic ABCs of Christian faith (see 5:12). They are spiritual babies, who "need milk, not solid food" (5:13).

These words of exasperation may serve as a reminder to us of the importance of continued nurture and growth to the vitality of Christian faith, lest we assume that "Christian education" is necessary only for children. Growth in faith is a continual process throughout our lives—with no graduation day in sight!

Continued growth occurs throughout our lives in a variety of ways:

1. As we carefully study the scriptures, the primary tradition by which we know who we are, whom we worship, and how we are to exist in the world as the body of believers;
2. As we listen to the "great cloud of witnesses" who speak to us through the confessions, hymns, and tradition of the church;
3. As we join together with other Christians in worship, service, study, and fellowship;
4. As we stretch our minds with programs of reading and Christian education;
5. As we reflect together on issues that face us in this world in seeking to embody God's purposes for human life.

An ancient churchman, Anselm of Canterbury, captured something of this reality in a famous phrase: "faith seeking understanding." If it is truly faith, Anselm insisted, it will seek to understand what is believed.

Indeed, it is important to note how the author of Hebrews tackles the dilemma before him. Although the sluggish Christians he addresses, in their arrested state of development, are ready only for "milk," it is his conviction that "solid food" is exactly what they need. People in this condition need much more than a pep talk. What they need is a deepened understanding of the person and work of Jesus Christ. Thus in 6:1 he urges them on toward "perfection," or maturity. He urges them to leave the "basic teaching about Christ"—the ABCs—behind and move on, with God's help (6:3), toward a deeper insight into the faith they profess. Solid food is what he offers, because this alone will revitalize their commitment to the faith.

He fears that if they do not move on toward maturity ("perfection"), and remain in their sluggish state, they will be in grave danger of falling away from the faith. Thus he appends a severe warning to his call to maturity:

> It is impossible to restore again to repentance those who have once been enlightened, and have tasted the heavenly gift, and have shared in the Holy Spirit, and have tasted the goodness of the word of God and the powers of the age to come, and then have fallen away, since on their own they are crucifying again the Son of God and are holding him up to contempt. (6:4–6)

These words (which are parallelled in 10:26–31 and 12:15–17) are the most disturbing words in all of Hebrews and have been a source of considerable discomfort for many generations of Christians, for they have often been held to deny the possibility of forgiveness for any sin committed after baptism or conversion. These words, more than anything else, led Martin Luther, the Protestant reformer, to an intense dislike of Hebrews and to a relegation of it (along with James, the Revelation, and Jude) to a later and less authoritative section of the canon. They have even led some Christians to put off baptism until their deathbeds!

Three things are critical, however, in any assessment of the severe warning in 6:4–6. First, it is important to note that Hebrews does not speak of sin in general but rather of the specific and extreme sin of apostasy, that is, the continuing, public, and defiant repudiation of Christ by those who have experienced God's forgiveness and newness of life. Hebrews speaks of a situation in which baptized Christians, for whatever reason, align themselves publicly with enemies of Christ. From the perspective of Hebrews, it is impossible to restore such people to repentance, for they bite the very hand that feeds them! They have cut themselves off from the one who is the source of forgiveness. There is no other means of salvation available than that which they have rejected.

Second, it is important to recall Hebrews' decidedly pastoral orientation. In 6:4–6 the author does not set forth a calm, reasoned, and definitive doctrine of repentance but seeks rather to address a serious pastoral crisis. He greatly fears that his weary readers are on the brink of disaster—on the verge of abandoning Christian faith. They must be made to see the gravity of their situation—the seriousness of what they are contemplating. Sometimes warning, rather than reassurance, is needed to bring us to our senses and alert us to danger. The author of Hebrews judges that this is not the best time for a reassuring affirmation that God's mercy is everlasting, though this be true.

Finally, it is important to note that the Christians whom Hebrews addresses have not yet reached the point of apostasy, for the author states quite clearly in 6:9 that "even though we speak in this way, beloved, we are confident of better things in your case, things that belong to salvation." In order to dissuade them from the course of action they may be considering, he holds before them the dire consequences. The severe words in 6:4–6 should therefore be taken as words of warning rather than of condemnation.

Hebrews reminds us that warning has an appropriate place in the life of the Christian community. In fact, as commentator Herbert Chilstrom notes,

> The tension between judgment and mercy is always a part of the church's responsibility. When we do not call people to account for their actions, when we water down the cost of discipleship, when we give false comfort to those who drift from the church and take lightly the discipline of worship and service, we do an injustice to the gospel. To give the impression that generous giving is optional, or that service to others is a mere matter of choice, is detrimental both to the hearer of such a message and to the church itself. There is plenty of room in the message of the church for rebuke and the call to repentance. There is room for a word of judgment. (*Hebrews*, 34).

However, as he also goes on to note, judgment without mercy is not gospel! The author of Hebrews knows this and thus announces good news as well. His tone changes dramatically in the verses that follow.

A WORD OF ENCOURAGEMENT
Hebrews 6:9–20

6:9 **Even though we speak in this way, beloved, we are confident of better things in your case, things that belong to salvation.** [10] **For God is not unjust;**

he will not overlook your work and the love that you showed for his sake in serving the saints, as you still do. [11] And we want each one of you to show the same diligence so as to realize the full assurance of hope to the very end, [12] so that you may not become sluggish, but imitators of those who through faith and patience inherit the promises.

[13] When God made a promise to Abraham, because he had no one greater by whom to swear, he swore by himself, [14] saying, "I will surely bless you and multiply you." [15] And thus Abraham, having patiently endured, obtained the promise. [16] Human beings, of course, swear by someone greater than themselves, and an oath given as confirmation puts an end to all dispute. [17] In the same way, when God desired to show even more clearly to the heirs of the promise the unchangeable character of his purpose, he guaranteed it by an oath, [18] so that through two unchangeable things, in which it is impossible that God would prove false, we who have taken refuge might be strongly encouraged to seize the hope set before us. [19] We have this hope, a sure and steadfast anchor of the soul, a hope that enters the inner shrine behind the curtain, [20] where Jesus, a forerunner on our behalf, has entered, having become a high priest forever according to the order of Melchizedek.

Hebrews rounds out the call to maturity on a positive, encouraging note. The author expresses his confidence in his readers and urges them on to the kind of faithfulness and love of which they are capable, as they have demonstrated in the past (6:9–12). Moreover, he expresses, in a nutshell, the purpose for which Hebrews was written and his greatest hope for his weary readers: "We want each one of you to show the same diligence so as to realize the full assurance of hope to the very end, so that you may not become sluggish, but imitators of those who through faith and patience inherit the promises" (6:11–12). He wants his weary pilgrims to keep marching, to keep moving, lest they fail to reach their goal!

To this end, he reminds them of the utter certainty of the promises of God (6:13–20). God's saving purpose for the world, begun in Abraham and brought to fulfillment in Jesus Christ, is sure and unchanging. Indeed, two "unchangeable things" guarantee this: the reliable word of God who has always been faithful, and the oath with which God doubly ensured it. This exhortation concludes, then, by reminding its readers once again that Christian faith and hope are based on realities outside the believer. They are based on the person and work of Jesus Christ, who has entered "the inner shrine behind the curtain."

Hebrews here introduces an image that will play a central role in subsequent chapters. We will soon see that in moving "behind the curtain," Jesus, our great high priest, has entered the inner sanctuary, the "Holy of

Holies"—which is to say that he has entered into the very presence of God. He is "a forerunner on our behalf" who leads us also into God's presence to share their communion. This is the objective reality on which Christian hope is based—hope that is "a sure and steadfast anchor of the soul" (6:19). This is the anchor that grounds us and steadies us and will keep us from "drifting" from the faith (see 2:1).

6. A Priest Forever
Hebrews 7:1–28

We are moving into the central section of Hebrews, which stretches from 7:1–10:19. The author now sets forth an extended exposition of the high priesthood of Jesus Christ. It is solid food indeed: The argument is elaborate and complex, and modern Christians are likely to find its ancient logic bewildering and difficult to digest! Still, we may appreciate the author's stunning conclusions and the innovation in early Christian thinking that they represent.

This central section of Hebrews may be divided into two parts. In the first part, 7:1–28, the focus in on Christ's eternal priesthood: He is "a priest forever, according to the order of Melchizedek." In the second part, 8:1–10:19, which we will deal with in the next chapter, the focus will be on the sacrificial act that is central to his office.

THE PRIESTLY ORDER
OF MELCHIZEDEK
Hebrews 7:1–10

7:1 This "King Melchizedek of Salem, priest of the Most High God, met Abraham as he was returning from defeating the kings and blessed him"; 2 and to him Abraham apportioned "one-tenth of everything." His name, in the first place, means "king of righteousness"; next he is also king of Salem, that is, "king of peace." 3 Without father, without mother, without genealogy, having neither beginning of days nor end of life, but resembling the Son of God, he remains a priest forever.

4 See how great he is! Even Abraham the patriarch gave him a tenth of the spoils. 5 And those descendants of Levi who receive the priestly office have a commandment in the law to collect tithes from the people, that is, from their kindred, though these also are descended from Abraham. 6 But this man, who does not belong to their ancestry, collected tithes from Abraham

and blessed him who had received the promises. ⁷ It is beyond dispute that the inferior is blessed by the superior. ⁸ In the one case, tithes are received by those who are mortal; in the other, by one of whom it is testified that he lives. ⁹ One might even say that Levi himself, who receives tithes, paid tithes through Abraham, ¹⁰ for he was still in the loins of his ancestor when Melchizedek met him.

We have already encountered several references to the high priesthood of Jesus in Hebrews (see 2:17; 3:1; 4:14) and thus have been alerted to the author's interest in this category as a key to the significance of Christ's person and work. However, one thing would seem to stand in the way of his contention, particularly for the Jewish Christians whom he first addressed. According to the law of Moses (Exod. 32:25–29; Deut. 33:8–11), priests were supposed to descend from the tribe of Levi. Moses' brother, Aaron, was the first high priest of the Levitical order. Jesus, however, descended from a different tribe: the tribe of Judah. How, then, can he be said to be a priest?

The scriptures themselves provide an answer to this question in the mysterious figure of Melchizedek, who makes only two appearances in the Old Testament. The author of Hebrews finds in the two Melchizedek passages God's own prediction of a new order of priesthood, superior to the Levitical line, and a foreshadowing of the priesthood of Jesus Christ. The first and key reference to Melchizedek is found in Psalm 110—a messianic psalm that permeates all of Hebrews (see 1:13; 5:6; 6:20; 7:17, 21; 8:1; 10:12; 12:2) and is central to the author's thinking. Verse 4 of this psalm would appear to anticipate the rise of a new order of priesthood:

> The LORD has sworn and will not change his mind,
> "You are a priest forever, according to the order of Melchizedek."
> (Psalm 110:4)

The author of Hebrews, convinced that Christ through resurrection now lives forever, sees no one else to whom these words could apply!

It is on the basis of the second and only other reference to Melchizedek, in Genesis 14:17–20, that the author of Hebrews then argues the superiority of this new priesthood in 7:1–10. Genesis 14 tells the story of a war that took place during Abraham's lifetime, when several kings from the east invaded the region around the Dead Sea and fought for its control, plundering and taking captives, among them Abraham's nephew, Lot. When Abraham heard of Lot's captivity, he mobilized his forces and pursued the invaders. Taking them by surprise, he freed the captives and recovered the stolen property. On his return from battle, he had a brief encounter with Melchizedek, who is described both as *"king* of Salem" (an early name, perhaps, for Jerusalem, long before it became the capital of Israel) and as *"priest* of God Most High." The priest-king Melchizedek blessed Abraham, who in turn gave Melchizedek one-tenth (a "tithe") of the recovered property.

The author deduces from this encounter that Melchizedek is superior to Abraham and thus also to the Levitical priests who descended from Abraham. That superiority is confirmed on two counts. First, Melchizedek blessed Abraham, and the author of Hebrews tells us, "It is beyond dispute that the inferior is blessed by the superior" (7:7). Second, though the Levitical priests are entitled by the law to collect tithes from the people, Abraham gave a tithe to Melchizedek, thereby acknowledging Melchizedek's superiority. Indeed, Hebrews playfully argues that "One might even say that Levi himself, who receives tithes, paid tithes through Abraham, for he was still in the loins of his ancestor when Melchizedek met him" (7:9–10).

Melchizedek emerges as superior, then, even to the great Abraham and his Levitical descendants. Moreover, he foreshadows the priesthood of Christ. Hebrews takes the surprising silence of the scriptures concerning Melchizedek's lineage, birth, and death to be a sign of his eternal priesthood: "Without father, without mother, without genealogy, having neither beginning of days nor end of life, but resembling the Son of God, he remains a priest forever" (7:3). Even the significance of his name, which is said to mean "king of righteousness" and "king of peace" (7:2), points to the one to come.

By means of the figure of Melchizedek, then, Hebrews is able to demonstrate that Christ is in fact a priest, though not a Levitical one. He is the eternal priest—the priest forever according to the order of Melchizedek whom the scriptures promised. In the words of Hebrews, he has "become a priest, not through a legal requirement concerning physical descent, but through the power of an indestructible life" (7:16)—resurrection life!

IMPLICATIONS OF CHRIST'S ETERNAL PRIESTHOOD
Hebrews 7:11–28

7:11 **Now if perfection had been attainable through the levitical priesthood—for the people received the law under this priesthood—what further** need would there have been to speak of another priest arising according to the order of Melchizedek, rather than one according to the order of Aaron? [12] For when there is a change in the priesthood, there is necessarily a change in the law as well. [13] Now the one of whom these things are spoken belonged to another tribe, from which no one has ever served at the altar. [14] For it is evident that our Lord was descended from Judah, and in connection with that tribe Moses said nothing about priests.

[15] It is even more obvious when another priest arises, resembling Melchizedek, [16] one who has become a priest, not through a legal requirement concerning physical descent, but through the power of an indestructible life. [17] For it is attested of him, "You are a priest forever, according to the order of Melchizedek." [18] There is, on the one hand, the abrogation of an earlier commandment because it was weak and ineffectual [19] (for the law made nothing perfect); there is, on the other hand, the introduction of a better hope, through which we approach God.

[20] This was confirmed with an oath; for others who became priests took their offices without an oath, [21] but this one became a priest with an oath, because of the one who said to him, "The Lord has sworn and will not change his mind, 'You are a priest forever' "— [22] accordingly Jesus has also become the guarantee of a better covenant.

[23] Furthermore, the former priests were many in number, because they were prevented by death from continuing in office; [24] but he holds his priesthood permanently, because he continues forever. [25] Consequently he is able for all time to save those who approach God through him, since he always lives to make intercession for them.

[26] For it was fitting that we should have such a high priest, holy, blameless, undefiled, separated from sinners, and exalted above the heavens. [27] Unlike the other high priests, he has no need to offer sacrifices day after day, for his own sins, and then for those of the people; this he did once for all when he offered himself. [28] For the law appoints as high priests those who are subject to weakness, but the word of the oath, which came later than the law, appoints a Son who has been made perfect forever.

The rest of Hebrews 7 reflects upon implications of Christ's eternal priesthood. Chief among them is the fact that there would have been no need for God to establish a new order of priesthood had the old one been effective. Clearly the Levitical priesthood proved inadequate to its task. Moreover, the establishment of a new priesthood calls for "a change in the law as well" (7:12), on which the old priesthood was based.

According to the law of Moses, priests were supposed to descend from the tribe of Levi—it knew nothing about a priest who was to emerge from the tribe of Judah (7:14). After such a priest emerged, the law was abrogated and revealed to be "weak and ineffectual" (7:18). Indeed, from Hebrews' perspective, the whole religious system of Israel, grounded in the law, falls under indictment. Hebrews is convinced that in Christ, God has provided a new way and "better hope, through which we approach God" (7:19). Moreover, Hebrews 8—9 will elaborate the claim that "Jesus has also become the guarantee of a better covenant" (7:22).

As we have noted, Hebrews is distinguished by a notable (and problematic) emphasis on the "superiority" of Christianity to Judaism (see pages 8–10). Indeed, Hebrews now proceeds to underline the superiority of Christ's eternal priesthood to the old Levitical priesthood with four final observations.

First, Christ's eternal priesthood, like God's reliable promise (6:13–20), is accompanied by God's oath, as Psalm 110:4 itself attests: "The LORD has sworn and will not change his mind, 'You are a priest forever.' " The Levitical priests, however, took their office without any such oath (7:20–22).

Second, Jesus' priestly work is not hindered by death: "The former priests were many in number, because they were prevented by death from continuing in office; but he holds his priesthood permanently, because he continues forever" (7:23–24). Consequently, he is always available when we need him: "He is able for all time to save those who approach God through him, since he always lives to make intercession for them" (7:25). Moreover, his ministry of intercession on our behalf takes place in a heavenly, rather than earthly, sanctuary (7:26).

Third, Hebrews notes that Christ's priesthood is distinguished by his moral character and by an astonishing sacrifice:

> For it was fitting that we should have such a high priest, holy, blameless, undefiled, separated from sinners, and exalted above the heavens. Unlike the other high priests, he has no need to offer sacrifices day after day, first for his own sins, and then for those of the people; this he did once for all when he offered himself. (7:26–27)

Christ's once-for-all sacrifice for sin will consume the author's attention in the chapters to follow. His is more than a "new and improved" priesthood; its permanent effectiveness brings an end to the need for human high priests. Finally, lest we forget, the great high priest whom Hebrews acclaims is God's own Son (7:28).

What are the implications of these claims for our own lives? While we must avoid the denigration of Judaism in our interpretation and use of Hebrews, we can certainly embrace the eternalness—the permanence—of

Christ's priesthood as good news! Change and impermanence are central realities of our lives that pervade our politics, economics, societies in general, and relationships in particular. On a personal level, a quick glance through my address book at the myriad changes of addresses recorded therein—both my own and those of my friends—is a sober reminder of the mobility and rootlessness that often characterize our lives.

What Hebrews announces, however, is that there is a permanent and unchanging reality on which we can rely: Jesus Christ, who, through resurrection, lives to represent our concerns before God forever! Even Protestants, who may not initially warm to the notion that they have a "priest," can appreciate the fact that there is one who knows fully the struggle in which we are engaged; who feels our hopes and joys, our heartaches and sorrows; and who brings them before God. Thus in those moments when we are too numb with grief or fear to pray, we can be confident that there is one who intercedes for us before the throne of God where, as Hebrews tells us, "we may receive mercy and find grace to help in time of need" (4:16).

He is always available—always on call! As Hebrews affirms, "He is able *for all time* to save those who approach God through him, since he *always* lives to make intercession for them" (7:25). Christ's eternal ministry of intercession on our behalf can be a stabilizing "anchor of the soul" (6:19), as waves of change wash over us.

A final implication is also worth pondering in connection with current debates about ordination. Christ, coming from the tribe of Judah, would have been ineligible for priesthood. As biblical commentator Marie Isaacs notes, this thought "may be of some consolation to those women who, by virtue of their sex, are barred from ordination in those churches which perpetuate the priesthood in their model of ministry" (Isaacs, *Sacred Space*, 223). Neither did Christ have the appropriate "credentials"!

Hebrews declares, however, that the ancient qualifications no longer apply. The literal Levitical order is no longer operative. Is it appropriate, then, to restrict the image of the priesthood in Christian ministry along lines of gender, race, class, or sexual orientation? Hebrews can no doubt inform the church's continuing discussion of this matter.

7. A Perfect Sacrifice
Hebrews 8:1–10:18

8:1 Now the main point in what we are saying is this: we have such a high priest, one who is seated at the right hand of the throne of the Majesty in the heavens, 2 a minister in the sanctuary and the true tent that the Lord, and not any mortal, has set up. 3 For every high priest is appointed to offer gifts and sacrifices; hence it is necessary for this priest also to have something to offer. 4 Now if he were on earth, he would not be a priest at all, since there are priests who offer gifts according to the law. 5 They offer worship in a sanctuary that is a sketch and shadow of the heavenly one; for Moses, when he was about to erect the tent, was warned, "See that you make everything according to the pattern that was shown you on the mountain." 6 But Jesus has now obtained a more excellent ministry, and to that degree he is the mediator of a better covenant, which has been enacted through better promises. 7 For if that first covenant had been faultless, there would have been no need to look for a second one.

8 God finds fault with them when he says:

"The days are surely coming, says the Lord,
>When I will establish a new covenant with the house of Israel
>and with the house of Judah;
9   not like the covenant that I made with their ancestors,
>on the day when I took them by the hand to lead them
>>out of the land of Egypt;
>for they did not continue in my covenant,
>and so I had no concern for them, says the Lord.
10 This is the covenant that I will make with the house of Israel
>after those days, says the Lord:
I will put my laws in their minds,
>and write them on their hearts,
and I will be their God, and they shall be my people.
11 "And they shall not teach one another
>or say to each other, 'Know the Lord,'
for they shall all know me,
>from the least of them to the greatest.

47

¹² For I will be merciful toward their iniquities, and I will remember
    their sins no more."

¹³ In speaking of "a new covenant," he has made the first one obsolete.
And what is obsolete and growing old will soon disappear.

9:1 Now even the first covenant had regulations for worship and an
earthly sanctuary. ² For a tent was constructed, the first one, in which were
the lampstand, the table, and the bread of the Presence; this is called the
Holy Place. ³ Behind the second curtain was a tent called the Holy of Holies.
⁴ In it stood the golden altar of incense and the ark of the covenant overlaid
on all sides with gold, in which there were a golden urn holding the manna,
and Aaron's rod that budded, and the tablets of the covenant; ⁵ above it
were the cherubim of glory overshadowing the mercy seat. Of these things
we cannot speak now in detail.

⁶ Such preparations having been made, the priests go continually into the
first tent to carry out their ritual duties; ⁷ but only the high priest goes into
the second, and he but once a year, and not without taking the blood that
he offers for himself and for the sins committed unintentionally by the people. ⁸ By this the Holy Spirit indicates that the way into the sanctuary has
not been disclosed as long as the first tent is still standing. ⁹ This is a symbol
of the present time, during which gifts and sacrifices are offered that cannot perfect the conscience of the worshipper, ¹⁰ but deal only with food and
drink and various baptisms, regulations for the body imposed until the time
comes to set things right.

¹¹ But when Christ came as a high priest of the good things that have
come, then through the greater and perfect tent (not made with hands, that
is, not of this creation), ¹² he entered once for all into the Holy Place, not
with the blood of goats and calves, but with his own blood, thus obtaining
eternal redemption. ¹³ For if the blood of goats and bulls, with the sprinkling
of the ashes of a heifer, sanctifies those who have been defiled so that their
flesh is purified, ¹⁴ how much more will the blood of Christ, who through
the eternal Spirit offered himself without blemish to God, purify our conscience from dead works to worship the living God!

¹⁵ For this reason he is the mediator of a new covenant, so that those who
are called may receive the promised eternal inheritance, because a death
has occurred that redeems them from the transgressions under the first
covenant. ¹⁶ Where a will is involved, the death of the one who made it must
be established. ¹⁷ For a will takes effect only at death, since it is not in force
as long as the one who made it is alive. ¹⁸ Hence not even the first covenant
was inaugurated without blood. ¹⁹ For when every commandment had been
told to all the people by Moses in accordance with the law, he took the
blood of calves and goats, with water and scarlet wool and hyssop, and
sprinkled both the scroll itself and all the people, ²⁰ saying, "This is the blood
of the covenant that God has ordained for you." ²¹ And in the same way he

sprinkled with the blood both the tent and all the vessels used in worship. [22] Indeed, under the law almost everything is purified with blood, and without the shedding of blood there is no forgiveness of sins.

[23] Thus it was necessary for the sketches of the heavenly things to be purified with these rites, but the heavenly things themselves need better sacrifices than these. [24] For Christ did not enter a sanctuary made by human hands, a mere copy of the true one, but he entered into heaven itself, now to appear in the presence of God on our behalf. [25] Nor was it to offer himself again and again, as the high priest enters the Holy Place year after year with blood that is not his own; [26] for then he would have had to suffer again and again since the foundation of the world. But as it is, he has appeared once for all at the end of the age to remove sin by the sacrifice of himself. [27] And just as it is appointed for mortals to die once, and after that the judgment, [28] so Christ, having been offered once to bear the sins of many, will appear a second time, not to deal with sin, but to save those who are eagerly waiting for him.

10:1 Since the law has only a shadow of the good things to come and not the true form of these realities, it can never, by the same sacrifices that are continually offered year after year, make perfect those who approach. [2] Otherwise would they not have ceased being offered, since the worshipers, cleansed once for all, would no longer have any consciousness of sin? [3] But in these sacrifices there is a reminder of sin year after year. [4] For it is impossible for the blood of bulls and goats to take away sins. [5] Consequently, when Christ came into the world, he said,

> "Sacrifices and offerings you have not desired, but a body you
>   have prepared for me;
> [6]   in burnt offerings and sin offerings you have taken no pleasure.
> [7]   Then I said, 'See, God, I have come to do your will, O God'
>   (in the scroll of the book it is written of me)."

[8] When he said above, "You have neither desired nor taken pleasure in sacrifices and offerings and burnt offerings and sin offerings" (these are offered according to the law), [9] then he added, "See, I have come to do your will." He abolishes the first in order to establish the second. [10] And it is by God's will that we have been sanctified through the offering of the body of Jesus once for all.

[11] And every priest stands day after day at his service, offering again and again the same sacrifices that can never take away sins. [12] But when Christ had offered for all time a single sacrifice for sins, "he sat down at the right hand of God," [13] and since then has been waiting "until his enemies would be made a footstool for his feet." [14] For by a single offering he has perfected for all time those who are sanctified. [15] And the Holy Spirit also testifies to us, for after saying,

> [16] "This is the covenant that I will make with them after those days,
>   says the Lord:

> I will put my laws in their hearts and I will write them on their
>   minds,"
> [17] he also adds,
>   "I will remember their sins and their lawless deeds no more."
>   [18] Where there is forgiveness of these, there is no longer any offering of
> sin.

We now come to the sacrificial act that is central to Christ's work as high priest. The author clearly considers it the heart of the matter—"the main point" that he is trying to convey (8:1). He is not the first to speak of Christ's death as a self-sacrifice for sins; other New Testament witnesses also make this claim (see Mark 10:45; Rom. 3:25; 8:3; Gal. 2:30; Eph. 5:2; 1 Tim. 2:5–6; 1 Pet. 2:24; 1 John 2:2). He is the first, however, to infer that the sacrificial act must have been performed by a priest. Thus Christ is presented in a double role as both mediating priest and sacrificial victim. A hymn gives expression to this insight, which is unique to Hebrews:

> Offered was he for greatest and for least,
> Himself the victim and himself the priest.
> (*Lutheran Book of Worship*, No. 226)

Hebrews combines rich and varied imagery in its effort to convey the significance of the sacrifice that Christ performs as high priest. The images emerge, however, from an ancient world that is strange and largely unfamiliar to modern Christians. For most, therefore, these chapters are the most difficult in Hebrews. It may be helpful, then, to unravel the complex imagery that is interwoven by repetition throughout this section. Three central images intertwine: that of the Day of Atonement ceremony, that of shadow and reality, and that of the new covenant. By examining each in turn, we will begin to fathom the main affirmations of this key passage in Hebrews.

THE DAY OF ATONEMENT

The Day of Atonement ceremony and the high priest's role in it provide the central imagery by which Hebrews conveys the significance of Christ's person and work. Only Hebrews in the New Testament draws an explicit connection between the Day of Atonement ceremony and Christ's sacrifice, and it is one that would not have failed to make a profound impression on Jewish-Christian readers. The Day of Atonement, of Yom Kippur, is even now the holiest day of the Jewish calendar. It is a day of fasting, prayer, and self-examination that seeks the reconciliation—the "at-one-ment"—of God and the people.

In ancient times, it was also the occasion for an extraordinary ritual, described in Leviticus 16. Once a year on this day, after he had made sacrifices for himself and for the people, the high priest entered alone into the inner sanctum, or "Holy of Holies," of the desert tabernacle (and later the temple)—the only time that anyone entered there. In so doing, he crossed a boundary into holy space—into the presence of God. There he performed an act of cleansing with the sacrificial blood that purified the altar and sanctuary, the meeting place between the people and God. These were inevitably polluted by human sin, threatening God's presence there. The annual act of cleansing thus eliminated obstacles to the relationship between God and Israel by removing the barrier of sin.

The author of Hebrews does not explain how sacrificial blood effects cleansing and atonement, and the ancient logic is not clear to us. He simply shares with his Jewish contemporaries the assumption that it does: "Without the shedding of blood there is no forgiveness of sins" (9:22). The sacrificial rituals and the Day of Atonement are accepted as means of grace, as the God-given way of dealing with sin and of maintaining the purity required of the place of rendezvous between the people and God.

So central is the Day of Atonement imagery to the argument of Hebrews that the physical setting of the desert tabernacle and the sacrificial ritual associated with it are described in 9:1–10 in some detail. However, the traditional imagery explodes when it is then applied to Jesus Christ. The work of Jesus Christ both corresponds to, and contrasts with, the work of the Levitical high priest on this annual occasion. Jesus, too, enters God's own presence with a blood sacrifice for sins—but with a difference. He enters "once for all" and with his own blood! The Levitical high priest "enters the Holy Place year after year with blood that is not his own." (9:25).

Indeed, the annual repetition of this rite suggests to the author of Hebrews that it could not effectively or finally deal with the problem of human sin. Jesus, however, is said to have

> entered once for all into the Holy Place, not with the blood of goats and calves, but with his own blood, thus obtaining eternal redemption. (9:12)

He presented *himself* as a sacrifice for sins. This kind of supreme sacrifice can be made only once, for it entailed Christ's death, and one cannot die repeatedly! Jesus' self-sacrifice is thus a final, sufficient, fully effective sacrifice for sin: "He has appeared once for all at the end of the age to remove sin by the sacrifice of himself" (9:26). No further sacrifices are needed!

From Hebrews' perspective, Christ brings the sacrificial system to an end, for his extraordinary self-sacrifice completely and finally removes the barrier created by sin and opens direct access to God. Moreover, as we consider two other images, we will see that Jesus' sacrifice is distinguished from those of the Levitical priests in several further important respects as well.

SHADOW AND REALITY

If the discussion in 8:1–10:18 is confusing to modern Christians, it is largely because it combines the Jewish Day of Atonement imagery with equally unfamiliar Greek imagery of shadow and reality. The concept of shadow and reality is borrowed from Greek philosophy, which held that visible things of this earth are mere shadows or copies of the true realities that exist on the heavenly plane. This worldview was quite influential in the Hellenistic world, and Hebrews draws upon it to convey that the work of the Levitical priesthood foreshadowed the priestly work of Jesus Christ that is of ultimate significance. Thus the Levitical priests are said to "offer worship in a sanctuary that is a sketch and shadow of the heavenly one" (8:5). Theirs is "an earthly sanctuary" (9:1), where sacrifices are regulated by the law, which "has only a shadow of the good things to come" (10:1).

Jesus, however, exercises his priestly ministry in a heavenly sanctuary. He enters "the true tent that the Lord, and not any mortal, has set up" (8:2). His is clearly a "more excellent ministry" (8:6), for his priestly boundary crossing takes place on a cosmic plane, as through death and resurrection he passes into the holiest place of all: "Christ did not enter a sanctuary made by human hands, a mere copy of the true one, but he entered into heaven itself, now to appear in the presence of God on our behalf" (9:24). His priestly work therefore takes place in the realm of "true being," of ultimate reality—in the eternal realm of God.

The Greek imagery, however, like the Jewish Day of Atonement imagery, explodes when applied to Jesus Christ. The significance of what he accomplished cannot be fully contained within a dualistic framework of earthly shadow and heavenly reality, for, paradoxically, Christ's heavenly sacrifice was decidedly earthly as well. It touched time and history and involved Christ's own body on a cross (see 10:5–10, 20). Indeed, Hebrews has emphasized that Christ fully shared our earthly, human experience and that it is in fact his real human suffering that qualified him to be our "merciful and faithful high priest" (2:14–18).

The Greek imagery of shadow and reality is every bit as foreign to modern Christians as is the ancient Jewish imagery of sacrificial blood. Even so, we are able to appreciate that it is the author's way of affirming that what happened in Jesus Christ is of ultimate significance for the life of the world and that his work has bridged the gulf between heaven and earth, between ourselves and God.

THE NEW COVENANT

One final image is woven into the discussion in 8:1–10:18 to interpret Christ's sacrificial death: that of the new covenant. It is introduced early in the discussion, in 8:6:

> Jesus has now obtained a more excellent ministry, and to that degree he is the mediator of a better covenant, which has been enacted through better promises.

Christ's death is thus to be understood not only as an atoning sacrifice but also as a covenant-inaugurating sacrifice. As an atoning sacrifice, it deals with past sins; and as a covenant-inaugurating sacrifice, it establishes a new and lasting relationship between God and God's people for the future.

This final image, like the first, is drawn from the scriptures, for Hebrews maintains that Jesus' sacrifice fulfills the prediction of a new covenant found in Jeremiah 31:31–34. The very fact that a new covenant was predicted suggests to the author of Hebrews that the old one was inadequate. Indeed, he concludes that "In speaking of 'a new covenant,' [God] has made the first one obsolete" (8:13).

The problem with the old covenant was that it was not able to produce obedience to God (8:8–9). The new covenant, however, established in Jesus' death, will accomplish what the old one could not, for it is founded on "better promises" (8:6). Jeremiah 31:31–34 is quoted in full in 8:8–12—the longest Old Testament quotation in the New Testament—for it spells out the nature of the new covenant and its better promises that find their fulfillment in the death of Jesus Christ.

It is apparent from this quotation that the new and better covenant differs from the old covenant in two respects. First, Jeremiah announces that it is an interior covenant, one that involves our innermost being:

I will put my laws in their minds, and write them on their hearts, and I will be their God, and they shall be my people. And they shall not teach one another, or say to each other, "Know the LORD," for they shall all know me, from the least of them to the greatest. (8:10–11)

Second, Jeremiah announces that under the new covenant, sins are effectively forgiven:

For I will be merciful toward their iniquities, and I will remember their sins no more." (8:12)

Hebrews maintains that the sacrifice of Jesus Christ brings about the new reality that Jeremiah envisioned, for as a result of his sacrifice there is now available a new and definitive experience of forgiveness at the deepest, innermost level of who we are. Hebrews speaks of this experience as a *cleansing of conscience* (see 9:9, 14; 10:2)—something the sacrifices of the old covenant could not accomplish (see 9:9). Indeed, the very repetition of the old sacrifices served as a continual reminder of sin (see 10:3).

Now, however, sin has been dealt with fully, effectively, and finally in the sacrifice of Jesus Christ, and we know deep within our hearts the assurance that God will remember our sins no more. Our sins are removed from our consciences, and a new relationship of intimacy with God is made possible. We can stand with confidence before God, live in faithfulness to God's will for us (for it is written within our hearts), and engage in true spiritual worship (see 9:14).

Though the prophet Jeremiah did not specify how the new covenant was to be established and forgiveness of sins effected, the author of Hebrews discerns a clear connection between the new covenant and the sacrifice of Jesus Christ. In 9:15–22, he takes advantage of the fact that the Greek word for "covenant" can also mean "last will and testament" and explains that just as a will does not come into force until a death occurs, so also is a death necessary for a covenant to come into force.

Moreover, he notes that "not even the first covenant was inaugurated without blood" (9:18). The author considers it self-evident that a covenant must be ratified with blood, especially one that promises a definitive experience of forgiveness (see 9:22). What Hebrews declares is that the new covenant is now in force, that it has been ratified by the blood of Jesus Christ. We now stand in a new and lasting relationship with the living God.

A covenant relationship, however, entails obligations for both parties entering into it. For God, it entails an irrevocable commitment to remember our sins no more. And since God's will for us in this new and enduring relationship is for our *perfection* and *sanctification* (see 10:14)—a reference not to moral perfection or saintliness but to growth in grace—the covenant entails on our part a commitment to live so as to fulfill God's will for our lives.

A cartoon that once appeared in *The New Yorker* magazine captures this reciprocal obligation in a comment on Luke's familiar parable of forgiveness, the parable of the prodigal son (Luke 15): "Son, this is the third fatted calf we've killed for you. When are you going to settle down?" Clearly, God's gracious gift of forgiveness and the new covenant relationship established in Christ's death have direct implications for our behavior—for the way we live out our lives. "So great a salvation" (2:3) demands an appropriate response on our parts, and it is to this topic that Hebrews, in its closing chapters, turns.

We have noted a number of times that the imagery and argument of Hebrews is drawn from the ancient world rather than from ours and that it is addressed to Jewish Christians rather than to Jews. In our day, it would be a misuse of Hebrews, and grossly insensitive as well, to declare to our Jewish neighbors that our experience of the grace of God in Jesus Christ renders their religion and their covenant with God obsolete (see pages 8–10).

Still, we may rejoice with Hebrews that the reality of human sin has been finally and effectively dealt with by the perfect sacrifice of Jesus Christ. We may rejoice that we need not be paralyzed by the guilt and power of sin. We, too, may approach God through Jesus Christ, find our consciences cleansed, and experience forgiveness at the deepest level of who we are. We may embrace the good news that God both forgives and forgets, thereby freeing us to grow in grace and get on with the business of living in faithfulness to God's purposes for human life.

8. The Endurance of Faith
Hebrews 10:19–12:2

Hebrews, as we have noted, is addressed to fatigued and beleaguered Christians, who find themselves weary in the Christian way and on the verge of abandoning Christian faith. Its author is convinced that if he can rekindle their vision of what God has accomplished in Jesus Christ and made available in him, there would be no thought of drifting from the faith. Thus he has taken great pains in 7:1–10:18 to set forth Christ's work as high priest, his once-for-all sacrifice, and the new covenant relationship established in his death.

His extended exposition now complete, he turns again to his readers to renew the call to faithfulness. Surely they will not fail to respond to "so great a salvation" (2:3)! If they have caught but a glimpse of the incomparable gift of God in Christ Jesus, they will remain steadfast on the pilgrimage of faith. As this next section of Hebrews makes clear, that pilgrimage requires perseverance and endurance, but faith empowers believers to endure, and the reward at the end of the journey is great.

Christians of every age would do well to attend closely to these chapters, for the issues of perseverance and endurance that they highlight are of perennial importance in an attempt to live out the Christian life—as old Screwtape knew. Indeed, C. S. Lewis's fictional satanic mentor readies his young devil for the fight against Christians with the following advice:

> It is so hard for these creatures to *persevere*. The routine of adversity, the gradual decay of youthful loves and youthful hopes, the quiet despair (hardly felt as pain) of ever overcoming the chronic temptations with which we have again and again defeated them, the drabness which we create in their lives and the inarticulate resentment with which we teach them to respond to it—all this provides admirable opportunities of wearing out a soul by attrition. (*The Screwtape Letters*, 143)

As we will see, perseverance and endurance are, for Hebrews, the essence of faith.

A CALL TO PERSEVERE
Hebrews 10:19–39

10:19 Therefore, my friends, since we have confidence to enter the sanctuary by the blood of Jesus, 20 by the new and living way that he opened for us through the curtain (that is, through his flesh), 21 and since we have a great priest over the house of God, 22 let us approach with a true heart in full assurance of faith, with our hearts sprinkled clean from an evil conscience and our bodies washed with pure water. 23 Let us hold fast to the confession of our hope without wavering, for he who has promised is faithful. 24 And let us consider how to provoke one another to love and good deeds, 25 not neglecting to meet together, as is the habit of some, but encouraging one another, and all the more as you see the Day approaching.

26 For if we willfully persist in sin after having received the knowledge of the truth, there no longer remains a sacrifice for sins, 27 but a fearful prospect of judgment, and a fury of fire that will consume the adversaries. 28 Anyone who has violated the law of Moses dies without mercy "on the testimony of two or three witnesses." 29 How much worse punishment do you think will be deserved by those who have spurned the Son of God, profaned the blood of the covenant by which they were sanctified, and outraged the Spirit of grace? 30 For we know the one who said, "Vengeance is mine, I will repay." And again, "The Lord will judge his people." 31 It is a fearful thing to fall into the hands of the living God.

32 But recall those earlier days when, after you had been enlightened, you endured a hard struggle with sufferings, 33 sometimes being publicly exposed to abuse and persecution, and sometimes being partners with those so treated. 34 For you had compassion for those who were in prison, and you cheerfully accepted the plundering of your possessions, knowing that you yourselves possessed something better and more lasting. 35 Do not, therefore, abandon that confidence of yours; it brings a great reward. 36 For you need endurance, so that when you have done the will of God, you may receive what was promised.

For yet "in a very little while,
      the one who is coming will come and will not delay;
but my righteous one will live by faith.
      My soul takes no pleasure in anyone who shrinks back."
39 But we are not among those who shrink back and so are lost, but among those who have faith and so are saved.

The word "therefore" in 10:19 signals that the author of Hebrews is once again ready to address the implications of Christ's work for the lives of his readers. In the renewed call to faithfulness that follows, he attempts in four ways to motivate and rejuvenate weary Christians for the pilgrimage of faith.

1. In 10:19–25, he first reminds them, once again, of what Christ has accomplished in their behalf, and with a threefold appeal urges them to take advantage of it:

> Therefore, my friends, since we have confidence to enter the sanctuary by the blood of Jesus, by the new and living way that he opened for us through the curtain (that is, through the flesh), and since we have a great priest over the house of God, let us approach . . . Let us hold fast . . . let us consider how to provoke one another to love. . . .

These verses capture in summary fashion the accomplishment of Jesus Christ set forth in 7:1–10:18. The "curtain" is that which separated the "Holy of Holies" from the rest of the tabernacle sanctuary—the one through which the high priest passed when he entered into the presence of God on the Day of Atonement only once a year.

By means of his sacrificial death (that is, "through his flesh," 10:20), our great high priest Jesus Christ has opened for us a way through that curtain. He has made available access to God! Thus that which was once the extraordinary privilege of the high priest alone, on only one day of the year, is now the privilege of every member of the community of faith.

A threefold appeal thus urges Christians to take advantage of Christ's accomplished work, an appeal that highlights the three great virtues of faith, hope, and love. The first appeal is to enter into God's presence: "Let us approach with a true heart in full assurance of *faith*" (10:22). We can come before the living God with confidence and know that we are accepted and embraced, not because we are inherently worthy of acceptance but because we have been "sprinkled clean" with baptismal waters—an external sign of the internal cleansing of our consciences from sin made possible by the priestly work of Christ.

The second appeal is this: "Let us hold fast to the confession of our *hope* without wavering" (10:23). Hope is directed toward the fact that God's purposes for the world, which have been realized in Jesus Christ, now move steadily toward their final fulfillment on the last day, when Christ's lordship will be recognized by all. Indeed the "Day" approaches (10:25). That God's purposes for the world will one day be fulfilled is certain, for God who is revealed in Jesus Christ is, above all else, faithful to promises.

The third appeal is both a reminder of the fellowship Christians share because of what Christ has done and an exhortation not to neglect it: "Let us consider how to provoke one another to *love* and good deeds, not neglecting to meet together, as is the habit of some, but encouraging one another . . ." (10:24–25). The admonition to "provoke one another to love" might seem odd at first glance. But it is important to bear in mind that love is not that emotion extolled in greeting cards as "the feeling you feel when you feel you're going to feel a feeling you never felt before." Love, in the New Testament, is not something you feel; it is something you do. The love of which the New Testament speaks seeks the well-being of others and is expressed in concrete efforts on their behalf. Indeed, it is modeled on the concrete self-giving of God in Jesus Christ. This kind of love can be commanded, stimulated, "provoked."

Hebrews notes that one of the primary ways in which we can stir up and demonstrate love for our fellow Christians is by "not neglecting to meet together," which had apparently become the habit of some of the Christians to whom Hebrews was first addressed. It is a bad habit into which many Christians still easily fall today. Church attendance may cease to be a priority, as Christians are sometimes tempted to worship at "Her Mattress by the Springs." But how can we encourage one another and care for one another if we neglect our fellowship? How can we experience the full assurance of faith or the confidence of hope when the pews are empty on Sunday morning and the fellow saints are home in bed?

As biblical commentator William Johnsson notes, Hebrews provides an answer to the question "Why go to church?": "because of what Christ has done, because of who we are, because of the opportunities for mutual encouragement and growth, and because of the times" (*Hebrews*, 76).

2. The second way in which the author of Hebrews seeks to motivate his readers is with a stern warning in 10:26–31, which repeats the dire warning in 6:4–8. He greatly fears that if they continue to "drift" they will be in grave danger of falling away completely from the faith, and he does not hesitate to hold forth the consequences. This warning has been every bit as troublesome to generations of Christians as the earlier one in 6:4–8 (see pages 37–38), for it too has been held to deny the possibility of forgiveness for any sin committed after baptism or conversion.

Again, however, it is important to note that Hebrews speaks not of sin in general, but rather of the extreme sin of apostasy—that is, of overt denial of Christian faith by one who has experienced the grace of God in Jesus Christ. That an overt, public, and continuing repudiation of Christ is in view is apparent from the language of the text: Apostates are said to "persist" in sin, to "spurn" the Son of God, to "profane" the blood of the covenant by which they were sanctified, and to "outrage" the Spirit of grace. A "fearful prospect of judgment, and a fury of fire" await such ones, not because God is unwilling to forgive but because they have turned their back on the very source of God's forgiveness by denying Jesus Christ.

Moreover, we should not think the author of Hebrews heartless for warning his readers of the consequences of such sin. Indeed, as commentator Herbert Chilstrom observes, he embodies what we have begun to call "tough love": "the kind of love that sets standards and absolutes, talks about limits, and lays down consequences" (*Hebrews*, 54). That he believes in them and hopes for the best concerning them is apparent from the encouraging words that follow.

3. The third way in which the author of Hebrews seeks to motivate and rejuvenate his readers is by calling to their remembrance their earlier history in 10:32–39. These verses of recollection provide our best glimpses into the life situation of the Christians whom Hebrews first addressed. It is apparent that at some point in their early history as Christians they had remained faithful during the most trying of circumstances. They had willingly endured public abuse and even "the plundering of their possessions" for their Christian confession and had supported their fellow Christians in the midst of suffering (10:34). The persecution of the Roman Christians by the emperor Claudius may be in view (see pages 12–14), but we cannot know for sure. Whatever occasioned their suffering, the point the author wishes to make is that if they endured successfully in the past, they can certainly endure in the present and in the future. They have proved that they are not "shrinking violets" (10:39). They are made of sturdy stuff indeed!

Thus he urges them not to abandon their confidence and boldness. Recollection of their past history can strengthen their faith. They are urged to look backward and then forward. The fellowship of the Christian community that sustained them in the past will sustain them in the present and the future. The God who provided for them in the past will provide for them in the present and the future.

Indeed, the second coming of Christ and the fulfillment of God's saving purposes may be just around the corner: "In a very little while, the one who is coming will come and will not delay" (10:37). Given their exemplary past history, the author of Hebrews is confident that they can persevere until that time: "We are not among those who shrink back and so are lost, but among those who have faith and so are saved" (10:39).

4. The reference to "those who have faith" in 10:39 leads, in chapter 11, to an extended excursus on the power of faith. That power is evident

in the lives of the saints of preceding generations, and their example will surely inspire and encourage weary Christians. This is the fourth way in which the author seeks to motivate his readers: by calling to their remembrance the "great cloud of witnesses" whose lives bear testimony to the power of faith. This brings us to Hebrews' most famous chapter.

THE GREAT CLOUD OF WITNESSES
Hebrews 11:1–12:2

11:1 Now faith is the assurance of things hoped for, the conviction of things not seen. 2 Indeed, by faith our ancestors received approval. 3 By faith we understand that the worlds were prepared by the word of God, so that what is seen was made from things that are not visible.

4 By faith Abel offered to God a more acceptable sacrifice than Cain's. Through this he received approval as righteous, God himself giving approval to his gifts; he died, but through his faith he still speaks. 5 By faith Enoch was taken so that he did not experience death; and "he was not found, because God had taken him." For it was attested before he was taken away that "he had pleased God." 6 And without faith it is impossible to please God, for whoever would approach him must believe that he exists and that he rewards those who seek him. 7 By faith Noah, warned by God about events as yet unseen, respected the warning and built an ark to save his household; by this he condemned the world and became an heir to the righteousness that is in accordance with faith.

8 By faith Abraham obeyed when he was called to set out for a place that he was to receive as an inheritance; and he set out, not knowing where he was going. 9 By faith he stayed for a time in the land he had been promised, as in a foreign land, living in tents, as did Isaac and Jacob, who were heirs with him of the same promise. 10 For he looked forward to the city that has foundations, whose architect and builder is God. 11 By faith he received power of procreation, even though he was too old—and Sarah herself was barren—because he considered him faithful who had promised. 12 Therefore from one person, and this one as good as dead, descendants were born, "as many as the stars of heaven and as the innumerable grains of sand by the seashore."

13 All of these died in faith without having received the promises, but from a distance they saw and greeted them. They confessed that they were strangers and foreigners on the earth, 14 for people who speak in this way make it clear that they are seeking a homeland. 15 If they had been thinking of the land that they had left behind, they would have had opportunity to return. 16 But as it is, they desire a better country, that is, a heavenly one.

Therefore God is not ashamed to be called their God; indeed, he has prepared a city for them.

[17] By faith Abraham, when put to the test, offered up Isaac. He who had
received the promises was ready to offer up his only son, [18] of whom he had
been told, "It is through Isaac that descendants shall be named for you."
[19] He considered the fact that God is able even to raise someone from the
dead—and figuratively speaking, he did receive him back. [20] By faith Isaac
invoked blessings for the future on Jacob and Esau. [21] By faith Jacob, when
dying, blessed each of the sons of Joseph, "bowing in worship over the top
of his staff." [22] By faith Joseph, at the end of his life, made mention of the
exodus of the Israelites and gave instructions about his burial.

[23] By faith Moses was hidden by his parents for three months after his
birth, because they saw that the child was beautiful; and they were not
afraid of the king's edict. [24] By faith Moses, when he was grown up, refused
to be called a son of Pharaoh's daughter, [25] choosing rather to share ill-treat-
ment with the people of God than to enjoy the fleeting pleasures of sin. [26]
He considered abuse suffered for the Christ to be greater wealth than the
treasures of Egypt, for he was looking ahead to the reward. [27] By faith he left
Egypt, unafraid of the king's anger; for he persevered as though he saw him
who is invisible. [28] By faith he kept the Passover and the sprinkling of blood,
so that the destroyer of the firstborn would not touch the firstborn of Israel.

[29] By faith the people passed through the Red Sea as if it were dry land,
but when the Egyptians attempted to do so they were drowned. [30] By faith
the walls of Jericho fell after they had been encircled for seven days. [31] By
faith Rahab the prostitute did not perish with those who were disobedient,
because she had received the spies in peace.

[32] And what more should I say? For time would fail me to tell of Gideon,
Barak, Samson, Jephthah, of David and Samuel and the prophets— [33] who
through faith conquered kingdoms, administered justice, obtained
promises, shut the mouths of lions, [34] quenched a raging fire, escaped the
edge of the sword, won strength out of weakness, became mighty in war,
put foreign armies to flight. [35] Women received their dead by resurrection.
Others were tortured, refusing to accept release, in order to obtain a better
resurrection. [36] Others suffered mocking and flogging, and even chains and
imprisonment. [37] They were stoned to death, they were sawn in two, they
were killed by the sword; they went about in skins of sheep and goats, destitute, persecuted, tormented— [38] of whom the world was not worthy. They
wandered in deserts and mountains, and in caves and holes in the ground.

[39] Yet all these, though they were commended for their faith, did not receive what was promised, [40] since God had provided something better so
that they would not, apart from us, be made perfect.

12:1 Therefore, since we are surrounded by so great a cloud of witnesses, let us also lay aside every weight and the sin that clings so closely,

and let us run with perseverance the race that is set before us, [2] looking to Jesus the pioneer and perfecter of our faith, who for the sake of the joy that was set before him endured the cross, disregarding its shame, and has taken his seat at the right hand of the throne of God.

Hebrews speaks of "faith" more than any other book in the New Testament. In Hebrews 11 alone, the word "faith" appears twenty-four times. However, Hebrews highlights a different aspect of it than do other New Testament witnesses. The apostle Paul, for example, speaks of faith as a passive reality: It is essentially trusting acceptance of Christ's saving work as a gift from God. What Hebrews intends by "faith," however, is closer in meaning to "faithfulness." It speaks of faith as active in obedience. It is that characteristic of the Christian life that enables one both to persevere even in the midst of difficult circumstances and to step out into the unknown with courage and live in a risky and vigorous way.

How so? Hebrews captures, in its most familiar line, the characteristic of faith that empowers this kind of living: "Now faith is the assurance of things hoped for, the conviction of things not seen" (11:1). Faith, in other words, means that there is more to this world than meets the eye! It means that this world of value and power is on its way out, for God is bringing into being a new world according to the person and passion of Jesus Christ.

Faith means that the world and its human community are destined by God for redemption and that even now all of history moves steadily toward that day when Christ will come again, and God's reign will be established in fullness: "a new heaven and a new earth" (Rev. 21:1). To this end we pray, "Your kingdom come, your will be done, on earth as it is in heaven." Faith is this "assurance of things hoped for, the conviction of things not seen" (11:1). It enables believers to live by a vision of the reality of God and God's purposes for the earth, a vision that is not yet present or visible to the eye. It empowers believers to move into the future with trust and confidence, knowing that the future belongs to God.

The power of this kind of faith-vision was articulated in a memorable fashion by the civil rights leader Martin Luther King, Jr. in his most famous speech, "I Have a Dream." In that speech he eloquently set forth the vision of racial harmony that he perceived to be God's intention for us all. King's speech and life serve as a reminder that faith-vision does not lead to withdrawal from the world. On the contrary, it empowers risky and vigorous living in this world. It empowers us to step into the unknown with courage, to invest ourselves at those points where God's future may be

struggling toward realization now, confident that God's redemptive purpose in the world will not fail to be achieved despite all appearances to the
contrary. Indeed, we have a foretaste of that future in the present as we
test it and claim it, and as God's design for our humanity becomes visible
in lives of radical trust and costly obedience.

To inspire and encourage its readers, Hebrews brings forth a parade of
saints who lived by just this kind of faith-vision, who knew that there is
more to this world than meets the eye. Their lives pointed to and embodied the reality of the unseen, for they stepped into the unknown with
the courage and confidence that flowed to them from the Lord of the future. Each is introduced with the words "by faith," which by the end of
chapter 11 has become a powerful refrain.

The parade opens in 11:4–7 with three heroes of faith from the earliest
chapters of Genesis who illustrate the meaning of faith active in obedience. Among them are Abel, who offered a sacrifice (Gen. 4:4); Enoch,
who walked with God (Gen. 5:24); and Noah, who built an ark in response
to God's command (Genesis 6—9). In each case, their faithful actions
proved that their lives were governed by the reality of the unseen God.

The central figures in the parade then appear in 11:8–22: Abraham and
Sarah and their family, whose lives were shaped by their vision of God's
eternal world and by confidence in God's promises. This vision and confidence empowered them to risk in this world, to step out into the unknown, and to overcome obstacles. Thus, by faith, they obeyed God's call
to leave their own country for the Promised Land, and so left security behind and ventured into the unknown. By faith, they trusted God's
promise of innumerable descendants, and "received power of procreation," even though "Sarah herself was barren" and Abraham "as good as
dead" (11:11–12). And by faith Abraham, when put to the test, was willing to sacrifice his beloved son on whom the promise of descendants depended, trusting that "God is able even to raise someone from the dead"
(11:19).

Though they never received a homeland, lived out of their suitcases,
and ate off paper plates throughout their days, they were guided in this
world by their vision of a heavenly homeland: They "looked forward to
the city that has foundations, whose architect and builder is God" (11:10).
They knew that what God ultimately had in store for them "transcended
security and prosperity in a parcel of real estate on the eastern shore of the
Mediterranean" (Hagner, *Hebrews*, 190). Thus "they confessed that they
were strangers and foreigners on the earth" (11:13). They embodied the
pilgrim lifestyle that Hebrews holds forth for all believers, for Hebrews

maintains that our life on this earth is to be viewed as a pilgrimage to a heavenly homeland.

We believers are therefore always strangers and foreigners on the earth, resident aliens who are "in the world" but "not of the world" (John 17:14–18). We seek to embody the life pattern of God's eternal world, which is our ultimate destination, and so make it real in the here and now.

As the parade of saints continues with Moses (11:23–28) and other Israelite heroes and heroines (11:29–39), it becomes increasingly apparent that faith does not ensure that the believer's life will be a bed of roses. It does not guarantee prosperity or success by the world's standards. Indeed, it was faith that empowered Moses to choose self-denial rather than privilege, to turn his back on the "fleeting pleasures" of life in Pharoah's court, and to identify with the suffering of his people: "He considered abuse suffered for the Christ to be greater wealth than the treasures of Egypt, for he was looking ahead to the reward" (11:24–26).

Neither should believers anticipate that faith will guarantee deliverance nor that it will shelter them from suffering. On the contrary, as believers are guided in this world by the vision and standards of God's eternal world, they inevitably encounter opposition and maltreatment, for the world is threatened by those who do not share its values, and it lashes out at them. Faith, however, sustains believers in the face of the world's hostility. In enables them to persevere in the midst of suffering.

This is vividly suggested in connection with the vast hoard of unnamed saints who bring up the tail end of the parade in Hebrews 11:32–39. Among their number are those "who through faith conquered kingdoms, administered justice, obtained promises, shut the mouths of lions, quenched a raging fire, escaped the edge of the sword, won strength out of weakness, became mighty in war, put foreign armies to flight" and also those who were "tortured," who "suffered mocking and flogging, and even chains and imprisonment," who were "stoned to death," "sawn in two," "killed by the sword," and who went about "destitute, persecuted, tormented" (11:32–38).

Clearly, the lives of the saints in this world are not always easy. Indeed, the world is "not worthy" of them. Still, Hebrews maintains that the saints of every generation are empowered by faith to endure suffering and even death if need be, because they know that their ultimate destiny is in the hands of the unseen God whose promises are sure and because they know that God's purposes will not fail to be achieved despite all appearances to the contrary.

Indeed, with the faithful of preceding generations, we continue to wait for, and move steadily toward, the world's ultimate redemption in Christ. We are one with them in waiting for the final realization of God's saving purposes. And because Jesus Christ and the new covenant established in his death represent the fulfillment of God's purposes, Hebrews maintains that the saints of preceding generations will "not, apart from us" who believe in Christ, "be made perfect" (11:40).

Thus the parade concludes in a stadium in 12:1–2, where faint-hearted Christians find themselves "surrounded" by this great "cloud of witnesses" to whom they are connected by faith. Those who have already run, now pass off the baton for the last leg of the race and gather in the bleachers to encourage the next generation of believers to run well. We, like the Christians whom Hebrews first addressed, are called to join the pilgrimage to the heavenly homeland begun with Abel and to "run with perseverance the race that is set before us" (12:1). We do so cheered on by the saints of preceding generations, whose lives bear witness to the power and endurance of faith.

Most important, we do so "looking to Jesus" (12:2), who pioneered the journey and who also stands at the finish line. He is singled out for our attention as a model of faithful endurance, for he "endured the cross," and by his sacrifice opened for us a "new and living way" (10:20) into the very presence of God. As the one who has provided access to God for us all and who empowers us, he is the "pioneer and perfecter of our faith" (12:2).

In four different ways, then, the author of Hebrews has attempted to motivate and rejuvenate his weary Christians. He has reminded them of what Christ accomplished on their behalf and urged them to take advantage of it (10:19–25): He has once again warned them of the grave dangers of apostasy (10:26–31); he has called to their remembrance their exemplary earlier history (10:32–39); and he has challenged them by parading before them the "great cloud of witnesses" whose lives bear witness to the enduring power of faith (11:1–12:2). Surely they will be bolstered and encouraged by his stirring call to faithfulness and will remain steadfast on the pilgrimage of faith!

9. Concluding Exhortations
Hebrews 12:3–13:25

The last two chapters of Hebrews are filled with final words of advice—concluding exhortations for its readers. They include one last perspective on suffering, one final warning against rejecting God's grace, and a quick sketch of the contours of the Christian life.

A PERSPECTIVE ON SUFFERING
Hebrews 12:3–13

12:3 **Consider him who endured such hostility against himself from sinners, so that you may not grow weary or lose heart. [4] In your struggle against sin you have not yet resisted to the point of shedding your blood. [5] And you have forgotten the exhortation that addresses you as children—**
> **"My child, do not regard lightly the discipline of the Lord,**
> **or lose heart when you are punished by him;**
> [6] **for the Lord disciplines those whom he loves,**
> **and chastises every child whom he accepts."**

[7] **Endure trials for the sake of discipline. God is treating you as children; for what child is there whom a parent does not discipline? [8] If you do not have that discipline in which all children share, then you are illegitimate and not his children. [9] Moreover, we had human parents to discipline us, and we respected them. Should we not be even more willing to be subject to the Father of spirits and live? [10] For they disciplined us for a short time as seemed best to them, but he disciplines us for our good, in order that we may share his holiness. [11] Now, discipline always seems painful rather than pleasant at the time, but later it yields the peaceful fruit of righteousness to those who have been trained by it.**

[12] **Therefore lift your drooping hands and strengthen your weak knees, [13] and make straight paths for your feet, so that what is lame may not be put out of joint, but rather be healed.**

Hebrews has been called "the epistle of sufferers" and rightly so, for it is distinguished by the attention that it gives both to the sufferings of Jesus and to the sufferings of God's people. This attention is clearly pastoral in nature. The Christians whom Hebrews first addressed had endured suffering in the past. They had done so admirably, willingly enduring public abuse, even "the plundering of their possessions" for their Christian confession, all the while supporting their fellow Christians in the midst of suffering (10:32–36). Suffering is also likely to be part of their future. Indeed, new threats of persecution on the horizon may well have given rise to the community's weariness and discouragement, and to the temptation to "drift away" from Christian faith. Thus in its closing chapters (chaps. 10—13), the author strives in four ways to motivate his readers to persevere in the midst of adversity.

First, they are reminded that the second coming of Christ and the fulfillment of God's saving purposes may be just around the corner (10:32–39). Given their exemplary history, the author of Hebrews is confident that they can persevere until that time and that they will receive a great reward: "We are not among those who shrink back and so are lost, but among those who have faith and so are saved" (10:39).

Second, Hebrews parades before them a great cloud of witnesses (11:1–12:2), past heroes and heroines of faith who were models of endurance amidst adversity and whose example may inspire beleaguered Christians to "run with perseverance the race that is set before" them (12:1).

Third, in the section of Hebrews that is now before us (12:3–13), Jesus, too, is held forth as a model of endurance to emulate in one's suffering. It is further suggested that suffering is to be viewed as divine discipline and training, and as such, a sign of God's love and acceptance.

Fourth and finally, in Hebrews' closing paragraphs, readers are called to identify with Christ and to share the abuse that he experienced (13:13–14). In all of these ways, Hebrews seeks to embolden Christians to persevere in the midst of trying circumstances.

With the third of these attempts (see 12:3–13), the author of Hebrews sets forth a new perspective of suffering by drawing a clear connection between the suffering of Jesus and that of God's people. Christians are called to "consider him who endured such hostility against himself from sinners, so that [they] may not grow weary or lose heart" (12:3). The example of Jesus' endurance in the face of hostility can inspire Christians to face bravely their own experiences of reproach and rejection. He is a model to emulate in one's suffering. Many of us, like those whom Hebrews first addressed, have not been tested to the limit as Christ was tested nor required to give our all: "In your struggle against sin you have not yet resisted to the point of shedding your blood" (12:4).

It is further suggested in 12:5–11 that just as Jesus, "although he was a Son . . . learned obedience through what he suffered" (5:8), so may Christians learn and grow through experiences of suffering. We ought not to think that Christian faith shelters us from adversity. On the contrary, suffering and being a child of God go hand in hand. This is because those who are guided in this world by the vision and standards of God's eternal world inevitably encounter opposition and maltreatment, for the world is threatened by those who do not share its values, and it lashes out at them. In particular, those who witness to God's call for justice and who work for change in this world can expect sharp opposition. In many instances, suffering comes our way not *in spite* of the fact that we are disciples but precisely *because* of it.

Nor should we think that experiences of suffering are signs of divine displeasure. Hebrews suggests that they are rather to be viewed as divine discipline and training, and as such, signs of God's love and acceptance. Just as human parents discipline their children in love, so does the divine parent discipline and educate us through experiences of suffering, "in order that we may share [God's] holiness" (12:10).

These affirmations in Hebrews 12:3–13 are not without difficulties. It could perhaps be argued that God's *perfecting* of the Son (2:10) through suffering, and God's *disciplining* of all believers through the same, borders on a theology of cosmic child abuse. But that would be a distortion of the author's intent. Moreover, it would be a gross distortion of these words to apply them to human experiences of suffering in general. It should not be said, for instance, that those who struggle with the reality of cancer are being disciplined by God through their experience of suffering.

Let us be clear about this point: Hebrews speaks not of suffering in general but rather of suffering that comes our way as a direct result of obedient discipleship and Christian witness in the world. It speaks of suffering that comes our way as a direct result of our commitment to Jesus Christ. Those who suffer for their identification with Christ can emerge from trying circumstances even stronger in faith and witness. In our day, Christians in mainland China and in the former Soviet Union bear eloquent witness to this fact, as they have emerged from long periods of state-sponsored persecution with resonant faith. They have much to teach the church at large about what it means to live in the shadow of the cross.

Whether we find ourselves in similar trying circumstances or face milder forms of social ostracism and public humiliation as a result of our commitment to Jesus Christ, Hebrews calls us to look to Jesus, to follow him as a model, and to trust that suffering in discipleship to Jesus shapes us in his pattern and makes us stronger in faith and witness. Weary or discouraged Christians of every age can be emboldened by Christ's example and by this assurance, empowered to "lift [their] drooping hands and strengthen [their] weak knees" (12:12).

FINAL WARNING AGAINST REJECTING GOD'S GRACE
Hebrews 12:14–29

12:14 **Pursue peace with everyone, and the holiness without which no one will see the Lord.** [15] **See to it that no one fails to obtain the grace of God; that no root of bitterness springs up and causes trouble, and through it many become defiled.** [16] **See to it that no one becomes like Esau, an immoral and godless person, who sold his birthright for a single meal.** [17] **You know that later, when he wanted to inherit the blessing, he was rejected, for he found no chance to repent, even though he sought the blessing with tears.**

[18] **You have not come to something that can be touched, a blazing fire, and darkness, and gloom, and a tempest,** [19] **and the sound of a trumpet, and a voice whose words made the hearers beg that not another word be spoken to them.** [20] **(For they could not endure the order that was given, "If even an animal touches the mountain, it shall be stoned to death."** [21] **Indeed, so terrifying was the sight that Moses said, "I tremble with fear.")** [22] **But you have come to Mount Zion and to the city of the living God, the heavenly Jerusalem, and to innumerable angels in festal gathering,** [23] **and to the assembly of the firstborn who are enrolled in heaven, and to God the judge of all, and to the spirits of the righteous made perfect,** [24] **and to Jesus, the mediator of a new covenant, and to the sprinkled blood that speaks a better word than the blood of Abel.**

[25] **See that you do not refuse the one who is speaking; for if they did not escape when they refused the one who warned them on earth, how much less will we escape if we reject the one who warns from heaven!** [26] **At that time his voice shook the earth; but now he has promised, "Yet once more I will shake not only the earth but also the heaven."** [27] **This phrase, "Yet once more," indicates the removal of what is shaken—that is, created things—so that what cannot be shaken may remain.** [28] **Therefore, since we are receiving a kingdom that cannot be shaken, let us give thanks, by which we offer to God an acceptable worship with reverence and awe;** [29] **for indeed our God is a consuming fire.**

As Hebrews draws to a close, its author issues one last warning of the dangers of apostasy, one last warning against rejecting God's grace. This final warning reiterates the dire warnings of 6:4–8 and 10:26–31 (see pp. 37–38 and 59–60), and it is equally severe. It, too, denies the possibility of repentance to those who abandon Christian faith. To illustrate this point, attention is directed to Esau, "who sold his birthright for a single meal," and later "found no chance to repent, even though he sought the blessing with tears" (12:16–17; see Gen. 25:29–34).

The author of Hebrews is greatly concerned that his readers, too, may resort to cheap sale of their birthright. With the prospect of suffering on the future horizon, they may be tempted to barter their blessings and abandon the faith. Thus he urges them to "see to it that no one becomes like Esau" (12:16). Indeed, they are to look not only to themselves but to every member of the community.

Christians have a responsibility for each other! Because the lapse of one member can have a detrimental effect on the community as a whole, Christians are urged to "pursue peace with everyone" and to "see to it that no one fails to obtain the grace of God; that no root of bitterness springs up and causes trouble, and through it many become defiled" (12:14–15).

This final warning, however, is coupled with striking words of assurance and hope that remind potential "Esaus" of the incomparable gift that God has made available in Jesus Christ. What would they be giving up if they were to barter their blessings? Hebrews 12:18–24 provides one last, climactic summary of the benefits of Christ's work. It takes the form of a final, grand comparison between Mount Sinai and Mount Zion—or, in effect, between Judaism and Christianity, between the old covenant and the new. Hebrews, as we have seen, is filled with comparisons of this sort and is distinguished by a repeated emphasis on the "superiority" of Christianity to Judaism.

This final comparison, however, states the contrast in the strongest possible terms. Mount Sinai, the place where the Israelites were closest to God and formed as God's people, is described as a place of terror, of stern commands, and of dreadful exclusionary holiness. There worshipers experienced an immense distance from God (12:18–22). Christians, however, have come to "Mount Zion and to the city of the living God, the heavenly Jerusalem" (12:22), which is described as a place of welcome, of joyous festivity, and of inclusive holiness. Mount Zion and the heavenly city are the ultimate destination toward which believers journey (see 13:14).

Yet the ultimate reality that Hebrews describes is in some sense already enjoyed in the present, in the midst of the journey itself: "You *have come* to Mount Zion and to the city of the living God" (12:22). As a result of Christ's work, believers come even now into the very presence of God and enjoy fellowship with God, with Jesus, and the whole heavenly world (12:22–24). As Hebrews has testified at length, such access to God is made possible by the priestly work of Jesus Christ, "the mediator of a new covenant," and by his "sprinkled blood" (12:24).

This contrast between Mount Sinai and Mount Zion, between the old covenant and the new, is vividly drawn and serves as Hebrews' grand finale. However, contemporary Christians must exercise caution in their interpretation of this comparison, for it is overdrawn and presents a caricature of Judaism as a joyless religion based on legalism, in which God is remote and unavailable. Clearly this is an exaggerated distortion of Jewish faith. We can understand how first-century Jewish Christians, in the midst of a difficult process of self-definition and differentiation, may have been motivated to claim superiority for their beliefs over the beliefs of their parent-faith and chief competitor. In our very different historical context, however, we can certainly rejoice in access to God that we alien, Gentile believers have come to know in Christ and to which Hebrews bears eloquent witness, without any accompanying denigration of Judaism.

Having reminded potential "Esaus" of the benefits of Christ's work, Hebrews urges them one last time not to barter these blessings (see 12:25–29). Those who reject such an incomparable gift cannot expect to escape God's judgment.

Finally, Hebrews reminds them that the gift that God has provided is secure! They have received "a kingdom that cannot be shaken" (12:28), which is to say that in the midst of a complex and changing world, Christians have something secure on which to base their lives and hopes: the reign of God, which has come into their midst through Jesus Christ and will one day be established in fullness on the earth. The decisive event in God's plan for the world has taken place, and even now God's purposes for the world move steadily toward their completion.

Thus, in the midst of impermanence, there is a sure reality on which we can rely: Jesus Christ, whom Hebrews describes as "the same yesterday and today and forever" (13:8). The affirmation of the unshakable kingdom that is God's gift to us in Christ concludes with a call to worship, which can be the only appropriate response: "Let us give thanks, by which we offer to God an acceptable worship with reverence and awe; for indeed our God is a consuming fire" (12:28–29).

CONTOURS OF THE
CHRISTIAN LIFE
Hebrews 13:1–19

13:1 **Let mutual love continue.** [2] **Do not neglect to show hospitality to strangers, for by doing that some have entertained angels without knowing it.** [3] **Remember those who are in prison, as though you were in prison with them; those who are being tortured, as though you yourselves were being tortured.** [4] **Let marriage be held in honor by all, and let the marriage bed be kept undefiled; for God will judge fornicators and adulterers.** [5] **Keep your lives free from the love of money, and be content with what you have; for he has said, "I will never leave you or forsake you."** [6] **So we can say with confidence,**

> **"The Lord is my helper; I will not be afraid.**
> **What can anyone do to me?"**

[7] **Remember your leaders, those who spoke the word of God to you; consider the outcome of their way of life, and imitate their faith.** [8] **Jesus Christ is the same yesterday and today and forever.** [9] **Do not be carried away by all kinds of strange teachings; for it is well for the heart to be strengthened by grace, not by regulations about food, which have not benefited those who observe them.** [10] **We have an altar from which those who officiate in the tent have no right to eat.** [11] **For the bodies of those animals whose blood is brought into the sanctuary by the high priest as a sacrifice for sin are burned outside the camp.** [12] **Therefore Jesus also suffered outside the city gate in order to sanctify the people by his blood.** [13] **Let us then go to him outside the camp and bear the abuse he endured.** [14] **For here we have no lasting city, but we are looking for the city that is to come.** [15] **Through him, then, let us continually offer a sacrifice of praise to God, that is, the fruit of lips that confess his name.** [16] **Do not neglect to do good and to share what you have, for such sacrifices are pleasing to God.**

[17] **Obey your leaders and submit to them, for they are keeping watch over your souls and will give an account. Let them do this with joy and not with sighing—for that would be harmful to you.**

[18] **Pray for us; we are sure that we have a clear conscience, desiring to act honorably in all things.** [19] **I urge you all the more to do this, so that I may be restored to you very soon.**

In its closing chapter, Hebrews quickly sketches the contours of life in the unshakable kingdom—life under God's rule. That rule touches our lives with amazing comprehensiveness, as the concluding admonitions in Hebrews 13:1–19 attest.

How is it embodied concretely in our lives? It is embodied, first and foremost, in the "mutual love" that Christians extend to one another (see

13:1). One ought not to pass too quickly over this admonition or to assume that it is an easy one, for the history of the church, as well as of our respective denominations and local communities of faith, suggest that loving one another may be one of the most difficult things that Christians are called to do! Our greatest difficulties and most painful disputes are often with those with whom we live and worship, whose foibles and follies we observe at very close range. Moreover, it is important for us to recall once again that love, in the New Testament, is not something you feel; it is something you do (review our discussion of 10:24). Love seeks the well-being of others and is embodied in concrete efforts in their behalf.

The love and hospitality that we extend to fellow Christians, however, is also to be extended to "strangers" (see 13:2). Hospitality was a critical matter in the first-century world, for the Roman roads were filled with travelers—among them the church's first missionaries—whose ministries depended upon it. The rule of God continues to be present every day of our lives in acts of graciousness that we extend to others, acts that reflect God's love and testify to God's presence. In extending hospitality to others perhaps we will find, like Abraham, that we "have entertained angels without knowing it" (see Genesis 18—19)!

In what other ways is the rule of God embodied in our lives and made manifest in our world? Hebrews maintains that it is present in our solidarity with prisoners—indeed, with all who are persecuted and maltreated (13:3). Hebrews' first readers had distinguished themselves in this regard (see 10:32–36), becoming partners with those imprisoned for their faith, and are now encouraged to continue such faithfulness.

The rule of God is also manifest when marriages are "held in honor" and characterized by fidelity (13:4) and when lives are kept "free from the love of money" (13:5). An appropriate attitude toward, and detachment from, our material possessions is possible when we embrace the fact that our ultimate security is anchored not in this world but in the unshakeable kingdom that is God's gift to us in Christ. Hebrews urges Christians to embrace the promise of God: "I will never leave you or forsake you" (13:5). Therefore "we can say with confidence, 'The Lord is my helper; I will not be afraid. What can anyone do to me?'" (13:6).

The source of our ultimate security and the object of our ultimate allegiance is articulated clearly in Hebrews 13:8, a verse that in many ways sums up the message of Hebrews: "Jesus Christ is the same yesterday and today and forever." Yesterday, as our great high priest, he presented himself as a sacrifice on our behalf. Today, Christ intercedes for us before the throne of God. In the future, he will return to bring the saving purposes of God to their fulfillment.

Christ's great faithfulness to us is unchanging, and upon it we may rely. Indeed, if we but focus on the constancy of that faithfulness, we will avoid being "carried away by all kinds of strange teachings" and "regulations" (13:9). Those to whom Hebrews was first addressed were apparently troubled by "regulations about food" of some sort. In our day, we too must discern whether new teachings that blow our way are faithful witnesses to and rearticulations of the sure and unchanging word that God, in these last days, has spoken to us by a Son (1:1–2).

In its closing admonitions, as it sketches the contours of life under God's rule, Hebrews also directs attention to the obligation encumbent upon Christians to remember (13:7), obey (13:17), and pray for (13:18) their leaders. Those leaders, both lay and ordained, who have been entrusted with oversight of the church at denominational, regional, and local levels, need the support, prayers, and partnership of the whole Christian community as they carry out their tasks.

Finally, the most striking of Hebrews' concluding admonitions appears in 13:10–16, which borrows one last motif from the Day of Atonement ceremonies. The Levitical high priest took the blood of sacrificial victims into the sanctuary, "the holy place," while the bodies of the victims were burned "outside the camp" in a secular space (Lev. 16:27). Similarly, Jesus, as our high priest, entered into heaven, offering his own blood, while the death of his body took place "outside the gate," on Golgotha, a godforsaken hill located beyond the city walls.

Hebrews thus urges Christians to follow the pioneer and perfecter of their faith outside the gate and to share in his suffering: "Let us then go to him outside the camp and bear the abuse he endured" (13:13). By means of this striking image, Hebrews suggests that our Christian pilgrimages are not to be confined to holy spaces—to the safety of the sanctuary. Rather, we are to follow Christ "outside the camp" into all the secular spaces of our world, where we may well invite the world's hostility and share Christ's suffering as we embody God's intentions for human life.

Christ's death "outside the camp" made every secular space potentially holy, and thus those who follow him are to claim every arena of life as God's own and subject to God's rule. In so doing, believers will inevitably share in Christ's suffering. However, there is hope beyond abuse, for our security and our destiny are not anchored in this world: "For here we have no lasting city, but we are looking for the city that is to come" (13:14).

As we journey toward that final destination, Hebrews calls us to share in Christ's suffering and also in priestly work, for we, too, offer sacrifice. The sacrifice that we are to offer is not a sacrifice of atonement but rather "a sacrifice of praise to God" and sacrifices of good works, "sacrifices [which] are pleasing to God" (13:15–16).

BENEDICTION AND FAREWELL
Hebrews 13:20–25

> 13:20 **Now may the God of peace, who brought back from the dead our Lord Jesus, the great shepherd of the sheep, by the blood of the eternal covenant,** [21] **make you complete in everything good so that you may do his will, working among us that which is pleasing in his sight, through Jesus Christ, to whom be the glory forever and ever. Amen.**
>
> [22] **I appeal to you, brothers and sisters, bear with my word of exhortation, for I have written to you briefly.** [23] **I want you to know that our brother Timothy has been set free; and if he comes in time, he will be with me when I see you.** [24] **Greet all your leaders and all the saints. Those from Italy send you greetings.** [25] **Grace be with all of you.**

Hebrews closes with a magnificent benediction in 13:20–21, which represents the author's final prayer for his readers. Because it contains Hebrews' only reference to Christ as shepherd of the sheep, as well as its only explicit reference to the resurrection (see page 17), we may suspect that the author makes use here of traditional language of worship that is already familiar to his readers. As we overhear his prayer, we are reminded that God, who was able to raise Jesus from the dead, can surely bring us, too, through the most trying of circumstances and make us "complete in everything good so that [we] may do [God's] will" (13:21). Moreover, we are reminded that what God has accomplished in Christ, "by the blood of the *eternal* covenant," will endure *forever* (13:20–21).

In a final postscript in 13:22–25, the author conveys bits of news and personal greetings (see pages 12–14) and appeals to his readers to "bear with my word of exhortation." Indeed, may the witness of this letter continue to rekindle Christian vision, to renew commitment, and to rejuvenate weary believers of every age for the pilgrimage of faith.

James

Introduction

The letter of James is one of the more useful and practical books in the New Testament. However, it has never been a very popular book, thanks in large part to Martin Luther, the great Protestant reformer, who disparaged James as an "epistle of straw." Luther's comments are the best-known criticisms of the letter, and the stigma of his condemnation haunts it to this day.

Still, if Luther and others have been less than enthusiastic about James, the reasons are readily apparent. Upon first reading the letter, one is struck by the glaring absence of central tenets of Christian faith. In particular, one looks in vain for any reference to the life and ministry of Jesus, or to his death and resurrection. There are, in fact, only two brief references to Jesus in the whole letter, which can be found in verses 1:1 and 2:1. James has more to say about Rahab the prostitute than about Jesus!

Moreover, the letter is short on grace and long on "works" and thus has had the misfortune of appearing to contradict the New Testament's preeminent apostle, Paul, who maintained that we are saved by grace through faith *apart* from works of the law (Rom. 3:28). For all of these reasons, Luther complained that James has "nothing of the nature of the gospel about it" and denounced it as an "epistle of straw."

At first glance, James is a peculiar letter. Misgivings about it are laid to rest, however, when one important fact about the nature of James is understood: James's letter is what interpreters refer to as *paraenesis*, or ethical exhortation, in the form of a letter. "Paraenesis" is derived from the Greek word *parainesis*, which means "advice" or "counsel" or "exhortation." Paraenesis is ethical exhortation, that is, instruction concerning how one ought to live. This insight is crucial for one's reading and interpretation of this letter, for the purpose of the letter then becomes clear: James is not trying to evangelize the world; instead, it is calling its readers to live the Christian life.

The letter of James is not a missionary document; it is an in-house document, a document for use within the church. Thus it should come as no surprise that James does not present the whole of Christian truth, for it is addressed to readers who have already heard the gospel and embraced it and who are very familiar with the central tenets of Christian faith. What we hear in James is the voice not of a preacher but of a teacher, one who is anxious to help believers see the implications of Christian faith for behavior—for how they live out their lives. This is the focus of James. James urges believers to apply Christian faith to every aspect of life.

James is not the only point at which one finds paraenesis or ethical exhortation in the New Testament. Paul's letters, for example, usually conclude with short paraenetical sections (see 1 Thessalonians 4—5, Galatians 5—6, Romans 12—14), in which Paul provides very direct advice as to how people who have embraced the gospel should live. James, however, uses paraenesis throughout—from beginning to end. As biblical commentator Sophie Law observes, the letter of James is "the most consistently ethical document in the New Testament" (*The Epistle of James*, 27). It is one of the New Testament's most persistent reminders that genuine Christian faith has implications for how we live our lives.

Indeed, James has been referred to as a "showcase of Christian living," and no aspect of our lives is too small to be placed on exhibit ("Editorial introduction," *Review and Expositor*, 355). The letter lifts up a remarkable variety of practical concerns, and readers will find that it is extraordinarily relevant and concrete. For example, have you ever put your foot in your mouth? Have you ever been tormented by the memory of words you wish you had never said? James has much to say about the awesome power of our tongues to heal and to hurt and about the importance of disciplined speech.

Have you ever felt like Norm from the television series "Cheers," when he says, "It's a dog-eat-dog world out there, and I'm wearing Milk-Bone underwear"? The author of James knows that life is not always easy. Thus one of the first things the letter holds before us is a perspective with which to face the real difficulties we encounter in our lives. Have you ever struggled with temptation? Of course, in our culture advertisers make temptation a virtue, or at least an acceptable vice. We are led to believe that if something is really good, it is also tempting, illegal, immoral, or fattening. The author of James knows, however, that temptation is not attractive and speaks of its destructive power in our lives.

Have you ever made a snap judgment about another person, perhaps on the basis of their dress, race, class, gender, or age? Maybe at times you have felt judged on the basis of your outward appearance. James, as it turns out, has the strongest castigation of discrimination in the New Testament. Discrimination, from James's perspective, is simply inconsistent with Christian faith.

In five short chapters, the letter of James discerns (among other things) the relevance of Christian faith to our speech, to our economic pursuits and business practices, to our experiences of trial and temptation, to our responses to discrimination and to people in need, and to our life together in the Christian community. James deals almost exclusively with the social and practical aspects of Christianity. It reminds us of the everyday problems with which we struggle and maintains that Christian faith touches every aspect of life, transforming routine pursuits into opportunities for discipleship.

By the time we reach James in the New Testament, we have already heard the gospel. We are already familiar with the central tenets of Christian faith. But believers do not live by theology alone. What do we do? How do we live? What are the implications of Christian faith for how we live our lives? These are questions that confront us daily and this is where James helps us out. This is the point at which James is one of the more useful and practical books in the New Testament. It is, indeed, a showcase of Christian living, and behind every exhibit, and implicit in every line, is the central theme of this letter: the wholeness and integrity of Christian life. To see that theme embodied in the life of the church is the letter's primary goal as well. James's hope, expressed in the opening verses of the letter, is that we may be "mature and complete, lacking in nothing" (1:4).

The letter challenges us to be persons of integrity, that is, people who are consistent in all we see, say, believe, and do. Throughout the letter, by way of negative example, the author draws our attention to the "double-minded person" (see 1:8; 4:8)—the person beset by double-vision, double-talk, double-face—and expresses a hope that we, by contrast, will manifest integrity of faith. From the first verse to the last, James calls us to behavior consistent with our convictions and inspires us to *live* our faith. Those who study it closely will find within that "straw" much nourishing grain.

THE NATURE OF
ETHICAL EXHORTATION IN JAMES

Three further observations about the character of James's ethical exhortation will help orient us to this letter.

1. The reader will first note that James is strikingly Jewish but also thoroughly Christian. Indeed, James is the most Jewish of all the New Testament writings. Distinctively Jewish concepts pervade the letter. For example, the letter is addressed to "the twelve tribes in the Dispersion" (1:1), and in 2:2, the "assembly" or congregation is referred to with the Greek word for what is literally the "synagogue" (*sunagōgē*).

Moreover, James takes a positive attitude toward God's law or Torah (1:25; 2:8–13; 4:11–12); it quotes the Old Testament as authoritative (2:8, 11, 23; 4:6, 5:11) and it lifts up Old Testament heroes and heroines, such as Abraham, Rahab, Job, and Elijah, as examples of faith (2:21–25; 5:11; 5:17–18). James also echoes the Old Testament prophets when it calls for conversion (4:8–10), when it attacks rich oppressors (5:1–6), and when it insists that believers take care of widows and orphans in need (1:27).

Yet while the letter is strikingly Jewish, it is also thoroughly Christian. Christian connections pervade the letter. Even though there are few references to Jesus, the references to him as the "Lord Jesus Christ" (1:1) and "our glorious Lord Jesus Christ" (2:1) certainly presuppose the resurrection. Moreover, James alludes to baptism in the name of Christ (2:7) and speaks explicitly of hope of his second coming (5:7–9). The Christian community is referred to as the "church" (5:14), and the discussion of "faith and works" in 2:14–26 presupposes some familiarity with Paul's discussion of this matter.

Most striking of all, however, is the fact that the letter of James is filled with echoes of the teachings of Jesus. Consider, for example, but a few of the remarkable parallels:

> But I say to you, Do not swear at all, either by heaven, for it is the throne of God, or by the earth, for it is [God's] footstool, or by Jerusalem, for it is the city of the great King. And do not swear by your head, for you cannot make one hair white or black. Let your word be "Yes, Yes" or "No, No"; anything more than this comes from the evil one. (Matt. 5:34–37)

> Above all, my beloved, do not swear, either by heaven or by earth or by any other oath, but let your "Yes" be yes and your "No" be no, so that you may not fall under condemnation. (James 5:12)

> And everyone who hears these words of mine and does not act on them will be like a foolish [person] who built [their] house on sand. (Matt. 7:26)

> But be doers of the word, and not merely hearers who deceive themselves. (James 1:22)

Blessed are the peacemakers, for they will be called children of God. (Matt. 5:9)

And a harvest of righteousness is sown in peace for those who make peace. (James 3:18)

Parallels between James and Matthew's Sermon on the Mount are particularly striking. Indeed, some commentators claim that the Sermon on the Mount in its entirety is paralleled in James. Whatever the case may be, it is clear that James is well acquainted with the tradition of Jesus' teachings. James, in fact, more than any other New Testament writing outside the four Gospels, is permeated by the thoughts and sayings of Jesus.

Thus, while the letter of James is strikingly Jewish, it is also decidedly Christian. The first Christians, after all, were Jewish Christians. The author of the letter was no doubt a Jewish Christian as well (see chapter 10 on the authorship of James). Thus he draws from his rich heritage and from varied resources at his disposal to instruct the Christian community in many practical aspects of its life.

2. James's ethical exhortation is decidedly theocentric or God-centered. To be sure, James is short on Christology (explicit reflection on Jesus Christ), but it is rich in theology (reflection on God). James points to God, for example, as the very ground of Christian existence: "In fulfillment of [God's] own purpose [God] gave us birth by the word of truth, so that we would become a kind of first fruits of [God's] creatures" (1:18). God's own word has been "implanted" in us (1:21), and it is "the wisdom from above" that God so generously provides (1:5; 3:17), God's own spirit that dwells within (4:5), that directs Christian living.

Indeed, James maintains that God is a gracious presence in our lives. Is there anyone lacking in wisdom? Simply "ask God," James advises, "who gives to all generously and ungrudgingly, and it will be given to you" (1:5). James notes, in fact, that "every generous act of giving, with every perfect gift, is from above, coming down from the Father of lights"—from the constant and ever-faithful God (1:17). "Draw near to God," James exhorts readers, knowing that God is eager to "draw near to you" (4:8).

Every aspect of Christian life of which James speaks is related to God. For example, why is it inappropriate to curse one's brother or sister? Because that brother or sister is made in the image of God (3:9). Why is it inappropriate to fawn over the well-heeled visitor to the Christian assembly and shuffle the shabby visitor aside? Because in dishonoring the poor, one dishonors those whom God has honored and chosen to be heirs of the kingdom (2:2–6). And why is it arrogant to assume that life consists of doing business and making money, and that human calculation can secure the future? Because the future is not in our control, and we do not know what it will bring. In everything, we are utterly dependent upon the living God (4:13–17). James assists us in discerning how we might order and maintain every aspect of our lives in the context of God's sovereignty, how we as Christians are to live in light of the rule of God, or kingdom, which is now present among us in the earthly and risen Jesus.

Biblical scholar Luke T. Johnson maintains that the theological linchpin of this letter is found in 3:13–4:10, where James squarely sets two alternatives before us and asks us to choose between friendship with the world or friendship with God ("Friendship," 166–83). Friendship, as Johnson notes, was not a casual affection in the first century; it was one of the most discussed and highly esteemed relationships. Friends were considered "one soul," which meant "at the least, to share the same attitudes and values and perceptions, to see things the same way" (ibid., 173). Furthermore, Johnson notes that by the term "world," James refers to ways of thinking and systems of values that do not take God's existence and God's claims into account.

So which will it be? Will we share the attitudes and values and perceptions of the world and live as though God has no claim on our lives? Or will we embrace the attitudes and values and perceptions of God and live in a manner that acknowledges God's claim on our lives?

James's target is the "double-minded person" (1:8; 4:8), who wants to be both a friend of the world and a friend of God at the same time, who looks to both God and the world for values and security. But James insists that these two ways of life are incompatible; they are mutually exclusive. Indeed, James states rather emphatically that "whoever wishes to be a friend of the world becomes an enemy of God" (4:4). This choice between friendship with the world or friendship with God is presented clearly at the midpoint of James in 3:13–4:10. Perhaps it *is* the very heart of the letter.

Whatever the case, it is important to recognize the decidedly God-centered nature of James's ethical exhortation. Why? Because the Christian life that James describes is demanding and could not be pursued on our own strength. This is the good news: It is *God's* own gracious presence and power and wisdom that makes it possible for Christians to live as James describes.

3. It is important to recognize that James's ethical exhortation makes considerable use of dramatic, exaggerated language. The reason for this is

apparent when we consider that James is an in-house document that is addressed to people who have already heard the gospel. Thus it seeks to remind us of what we already know and to encourage us to do what we already know we should. For this purpose the author of James uses vivid, even exaggerated language and illustrations to grab us by the lapels and wake us to the implications of Christian faith.

The reader will quickly note that James's language is often that of hyperbole, or exaggeration. In 1:2, for example, the author recommends a remarkable response to unexpected trouble: "My brothers and sisters, whenever you face trials of any kind, *consider it nothing but joy.*" Consider trials nothing but joy? And in 1:5–6, the author advises: "If any of you is lacking in wisdom, ask God, who gives to all generously and ungrudgingly, and it will be given you. But ask in faith, *never doubting,* for the one who doubts is like a wave in the sea, driven and tossed by the wind." Never doubting? Is this possible, we wonder? Or consider the question raised in 2:15–16: "If a brother or sister is naked and lacks daily food, and one of you says to them, 'Go in peace; keep warm and eat your fill,' and yet you do not supply their bodily needs, what is the good of that?" A "brother" or "sister" is a member of one's congregation, and can you image that you would encounter a member of your congregation who is naked and fail to take notice? Verses 2:1–5, then, offer a striking exaggeration of the contrasting treatment given to the rich and the poor.

As a final example, consider the description of the tongue in James 3. In 3:7–8, for instance, James observes that "every species of beast and bird, or reptile and sea creature, can be tamed and has been tamed by the human species, but *no one can tame the tongue*—a restless evil, full of deadly poison." No one can tame it? Given the enormous attention devoted to the tongue throughout the letter, we may presume that the author clearly wants us to try! Indeed, the author of James employs vivid and exaggerated imagery to impress upon us the dangerous potential of the tongue in hope that we will make every effort to check it—to do precisely what James says is impossible to do!

Thus one should not take James's dramatic language too literally, without recognizing the purpose that is at work: The author again seeks to remind us of what we already know and encourages us to do what we already know we should. By using exaggerated language and imagery, the author of James seeks to grasp our attention and goad us into action.

This very effective teaching technique was similarly employed by the contemporary Christian writer Flannery O'Connor, whose "southern

Gothic" stories were often filled with bizarre situations and characters. When asked about this characteristic of her fiction, O'Connor replied, "For the hard-of-hearing you shout, and for the blind you draw large and startling figures." It is important to recognize this technique as a distinguishing feature of James as well!

10. Author and Audience
James 1:1

1:1 James, a servant of God and of the Lord Jesus Christ, To the twelve tribes in the Dispersion: Greetings.

WHO IS THE AUTHOR?

Who is the author who speaks to us through this challenging letter? We don't know! In the opening verse of the letter, the author is identified simply as "James, a servant of God and of the Lord Jesus Christ" (1:1). "James" is one of the most common of Jewish and Christian names. Indeed, there are five individuals named "James," mentioned elsewhere in the New Testament, who are likely candidates:

1. James, the son of Zebedee (Mark 1:19; 3:17 and par.; Acts 12:2)
2. James, the father of Jude (Luke 6:16; Acts 1:13)
3. James, the son of Alphaeus (Mark 3:18 and par.)
4. James the younger (Mark 15:40)
5. James the brother of Jesus (Mark 6:3 and par.; 1 Cor. 15:7; Gal. 1:19; 2:9, 12; Acts 12:17; 15:13; 21:18; Jude 1)

Church tradition has attributed the letter to the final and best-known candidate: James the brother of the Lord and the leader of the early Christian community in Jerusalem. However, the author nowhere identifies himself as a leader of the church nor as a relative of Jesus. Did James of Jerusalem in fact write this letter?

Some interpreters maintain that he did, since what is known of James of Jerusalem is consistent with the character of the letter. According to historians, this James was a dedicated advocate of Jewish-Christian piety who attached great importance to observance of the Jewish law. Since he was martyred in 62 C.E., his authorship would make the letter of James one of the earliest writings of the New Testament.

Many interpreters, however, are not persuaded that James of Jerusalem wrote the letter. Indeed, a number of factors argue against it:

1. The letter is written in relatively polished and literary Greek. There is some question as to whether the cultured language of the letter would have been in the command of James of Jerusalem, an Aramaic-speaking Palestinian Jew.

2. Nowhere does the author indicate that he is the Lord's brother or that he knew Jesus personally. One wonders why a Christian with such a special relationship with the Lord would make such scant reference to him.

3. The discussion of "faith" and "works" in 2:14–26 seems to presuppose Paul's theological activity. In fact, as we will see, James's discussion seems to stand at some distance from the resolution of Paul's struggle with this issue in the mid-50s of the first century and to be a response to a popular misunderstanding of Paul's position.

4. One of the most serious objections to James of Jerusalem's authorship concerns the letter's view of the law. James of Jerusalem's well-known devotion to the Jewish law placed great importance on cultic-ritual matters, such as circumcision, sabbath observance, table fellowship, and purification laws (see Acts 15:13–21; 21:18–24; Gal. 2:12)—matters that are never mentioned in the letter of James. The letter's own appeal to the law, or Torah, is limited to the Ten Commandments and the "law of love" in Leviticus 19:18 (see James 2:8–11). In other words, when the letter of James speaks of the law, it refers not to cultic-ritual observations but to the moral teachings of the Torah.

5. Finally, it was only slowly and in the face of opposition that the letter of James came to be included in the Christian canon in the earliest centuries of the church. Its late acceptance as one of the New Testament scriptures was due to doubts about its apostolic authorship. Thus, early on, the letter does not appear to have been universally regarded as the work of the Lord's brother.

For all of these reasons, a majority of interpreters think that the author is writing under a pseudonym or alias, that is, writing in the name of someone else. In this case he is using the name of James, the revered leader of the Jerusalem church, and associating his teaching with James's tradition and authority. It is important to remind ourselves that there were no shady connotations associated with this practice! We cannot impose our modern notions of intellectual property and copyright laws on first-century writings. Writing under a pseudonym was a common, acceptable practice in ancient times. It was a way of honoring that person and claiming to stand in the same tradition.

Thus while it is impossible to date the letter with any certainty, it is generally thought to have been written toward the end of the first century, well after Paul's activity in the mid-50s and after the death of James of Jerusalem in 62—at a time when the martyred James of Jerusalem had become a revered figure of the past.

Whatever the case may be, we know for certain that the author was a teacher. James 3:1 provides our only clue: "Not many of you should become teachers, my brothers and sisters, for you know that *we who teach* will be judged with greater strictness." The author is an early Christian teacher, one who was responsible for guiding the early Christian community in many aspects of its life. In fact, the letter of James may serve as an example of the work of early Christian teachers (see Eph. 4:11–13).

However, in the opening verse of the letter, the author refers to himself simply and humbly as a "servant," thereby giving expression only to his commitment, obedience, and loyalty to the God who has been made known in Jesus Christ. His specific identity will probably continue to be a matter of debate, and there is room for disagreement in this matter. But fortunately, while his identity is shrouded in mystery, one thing—the most important thing—is quite clear: his message for us today!

TO WHOM IS THE LETTER OF JAMES ADDRESSED?

Neither can we say with certainty to whom the letter of James was first addressed. The church has regarded James as one of the "general," or "catholic" (that is, universal), epistles. These epistles are not like Paul's letters, which are addressed to specific congregations and places—to the churches in Galatia, Thessalonica, Philippi, or Rome. The general epistles, such as James, Jude, and 1 and 2 Peter, carry the name of the author rather than of the recipients, because they appear to be addressed to Christians in general rather than to a specific community at a particular place. They appear to have been written for general distribution and to address issues in the wider church.

The opening verse of the letter of James, for example, greets "the twelve tribes in the Dispersion" (1:1). The "twelve tribes" is a way of referring to the Jewish nation, and Jews in the "Dispersion" lived outside of Palestine, scattered among the nations. "The twelve tribes in the Dispersion," however, is very likely a reference to all Christians as heirs of the Jewish tradition, for the early Christians viewed themselves as such and freely applied Jewish titles to themselves.

James, therefore, addresses a large audience: the whole of God's people scattered throughout the world! It speaks of general rather than particular situations. However, the discussion that follows does relate to actual history, in that it indicates those areas of life in the early Christian community that the author found to be most urgently in need of direction and regulation.

The areas of Christian life to which James devotes attention continue to be those areas that are urgently in need of direction and regulation today. This first-century letter is startlingly relevant in our century. In fact, a word of warning is in order: James is strong medicine, which we may find hard to swallow at some points! James hits close to home, for many of the defects the author discerns in his churches are found in contemporary churches as well.

However, if we carefully attend to this letter, James could accomplish a renewing of our Christian lives. Indeed, it has been observed that if the powerful social "message of James is allowed to go out unmuffled, it will rattle the stained glass windows" (Jones, "Approaches," 426). May James rattle our cages and renew us for years to come!

11. Trials and Temptations
James 1:2–18

Bad things happen to good people, and Christianity does not shelter one from the difficulties and tragedies of life. Christians share in the realities of pain, injury, loss, and sometimes oppression, which are the common lot of human experience. The author of James is keenly aware that experiences of suffering can provoke crises of faith. Thus the first thing he holds before us is a perspective with which to face the difficulties and tragedies of human life.

A PERSPECTIVE ON TRIALS
James 1:2–4

> 1:2 **My brothers and sisters, whenever you face trials of any kind, consider it nothing but joy,** [3] **because you know that the testing of your faith produces endurance;** [4] **and let endurance have its full effect, so that you may be mature and complete, lacking in nothing.**

"Consider it nothing but joy," James counsels Christian sisters and brothers, "whenever you face trials of any kind." The trials envisioned are not specifically identified. They are deliberately referred to as "trials of any kind." Whatever their nature, they are to be considered "joy."

What exactly is James advising? Is it promoting a martyr complex? Are Christians actually to take pleasure in suffering? Certainly not! The various trials that we encounter—experiences of pain, loss, injury, or oppression—are not at all occasions of joy in and of themselves. Such experiences are not to be sought; nor are they to be avoided or regarded as foreign to Christian faith.

The joy of which James speaks results from the growth that trials can bring. In the midst of them, we can be drawn closer to God, experience God's sustaining power, and grow in faith and maturity. James rejoices not in trials themselves but in the steadfastness of faith and integrity of character that result from experiences of suffering. Indeed, James says not a word about *why* we face trials or from *whence* they come. The focus, instead, is on where they may lead.

James points to the joyful consequences of trial, noting first that the testing of faith produces "endurance." James envisions an active steadfastness in the face of trial, not passive resignation. Passive submission to trials is not at all proposed, but rather an active, militant perseverance. In fact, Job is held up as a model of endurance in 5:11—the Old Testament person of faith who agonizes over his predicament and struggles bitterly with his pain before friends and the Almighty but who nevertheless clings tenaciously to God and refuses to yield to atheism. Such perseverance—such steadfast, heroic constancy of faith—is precisely what James views as one of the joyful consequences of trial.

Endurance, however, is not the final result of trial: "Let endurance have its full effect, so that you may be mature and complete, lacking in nothing." Here at the beginning of the letter is James's central theme and primary goal: the wholeness and integrity of Christian life. Trials can serve this end, for Christian life matures as the difficulties and tragedies of life are encountered, as faith "flexes its muscles under pressure." This is why trials can be considered "joy"—not because they are joyous in and of themselves but because endurance of them yields integrity and wholeness of Christian character.

PRAYER IN THE MIDST OF TRIALS
James 1:5–8

> 1:5 **If any of you is lacking in wisdom, ask God, who gives to all generously and ungrudgingly, and it will be given you. ⁶ But ask in faith, never doubting, for the one who doubts is like a wave of the sea, driven and tossed by the wind; ⁷,⁸ for the doubter, being double-minded and unstable in every way, must not expect to receive anything from the Lord.**

Divine wisdom may be needed to embrace this perspective on trials and persevere in the midst of them. It is available for the asking from God, who is a gracious partner in human life, "who gives to all generously and ungrudgingly." But the one who prays for the gift of wisdom must "ask in faith, never doubting"—with unwavering confidence in God's generosity and love and with certainty that God will answer one's prayer.

"Double-minded persons," who approach God with divided hearts and doubtful minds, "must not expect to receive anything from the Lord." Their hesitancy in asking stands in contrast to God's complete lack of hesitancy in giving. Moreover, the doubter's indecisiveness, or "double-mindedness," stands in contrast to the wholeness and integrity that is James's hope for Christian life.

POVERTY AND RICHES
James 1:9–11

1:9 Let the believer who is lowly boast in being raised up, [10] and the rich in being brought low, because the rich will disappear like a flower in the field. [11] For the sun rises with its scorching heat and withers the field; its flower falls, and its beauty perishes. It is the same way with the rich; in the midst of a busy life, they will wither away.

It may be no coincidence that James's first reference to poverty and riches is juxtaposed with words about experiences of trial. Indeed, a close reading of this letter suggests that economic hardship may have been among the chief trials with which James's first readers struggled (see 2:1–7, 24–27; 4:13–5:6). Here, James's words aim primarily to offer encouragement to the lowly "believer" in the midst of such hardship. Interestingly, the "rich" are not explicitly referred to as "believers"! (See my comments on 4:13–5:7).

GOD'S ROLE IN
TRIALS AND TEMPTATIONS
James 1:12–18

1:12 Blessed is anyone who endures temptation. Such a one has stood the test and will receive the crown of life that the Lord has promised to those who love him. [13] No one, when tempted, should say, "I am being tempted by God"; for God cannot be tempted by evil and he himself tempts no one. [14] But one is tempted by one's own desire, being lured and enticed by it; [15] then, when that desire has conceived, it gives birth to sin, and that sin, when it is fully grown, gives birth to death. [16] Do not be deceived, my beloved.

[17] Every generous act of giving, with every perfect gift, is from above, coming down from the Father of lights, with whom there is no variation or

shadow due to change. [18] In fulfillment of his own purpose he gave us birth by the word of truth, so that we would become a kind of first fruits of his creatures.

James's discussion on trials continues, but another element is introduced. While joyful consequences of trials accrue to believers in the present (1:2–4), James now adds to this the prospect of future reward. Those who endure trials may also rejoice that they will share in the life of the age to come.

A further dimension of trial is developed in the verses that follow. The author uses the same Greek word *peirasmos*, which can be rendered as "trial" or "temptation." James now turns from the external pressures that we endure ("trials") to the internal impulses to sin ("temptations"). And what is it that draws us to sin? Make no mistake about it: Temptation is not to be blamed on God! There is nobody to blame but ourselves. We are tempted, lured, and enticed to sin *not* by God but by our own desire. James describes the dreadful consequences of desire: "When that desire has conceived, it gives birth to sin, and that sin, when it is fully grown, gives birth to death."

Far from leading us into sin and death, God wishes to lead us into life. James underlines this fact by drawing attention to the good gifts that come from God and to the constancy of God's goodness and love: "Every generous act of giving, with every perfect gift, is from above, coming down from the Father of lights, with whom there is no variation or shadow due to change." James draws on a creation metaphor (that is, figurative expression) in referring to God as the "Father of lights"—the creator of the stars. First-century people observed with keen interest the movements of the heavenly bodies and their waxing and waning. James affirms that their creator and governor is exalted above any such change. Unlike the created heavenly bodies that shift in position and are darkened by the shadows of eclipse, God neither changes nor is changed by anything outside God's own self. As a familiar hymn, "Great is Thy Faithfulness," puts it, "there is no shadow of turning with thee." For this reason, it cannot be said that God, the giver of good gifts, could also inflict evils upon us (such as temptation). Such change would be contrary to the nature of God, whose constancy is one of goodness and love.

James rests this case by providing a premier example of God's goodness: "In fulfillment of [God's] own purpose [God] gave us birth by the word of truth, so that we would become a kind of first fruits of [God's] creatures." James refers to the rebirth, or conversion, of Christians, who have been "given birth" by the "word of truth" ("the gospel" in Col. 1:5) and who are "a kind of first fruits," or foretaste, of the redemption of the whole created order that is to come. The life that God benevolently "brings forth" for us stands in marked contrast to the destruction "brought forth" by our own desire and sin. James states unambiguously that God's constant, unchanging will for us is not trial or temptation, but life—a life of steadfast faith and wholeness, and in the end, life eternal—a life of constancy and integrity, which is modeled on the very constancy and integrity of God.

12. Hear and Do the Word
James 1:19–27

As the popular novelist and theologian Frederick Buechner observes, many people think of religion as "a good thing, like social security and regular exercise," but not "something to go overboard about" (*Telling the Truth*, 51). But to James's way of thinking, religion is not a casual matter. It calls for serious commitment, both in terms of careful "hearing" and faithful "doing." In 1:19–27, we are challenged to respond to God's word.

RECEIVING THE WORD
James 1:19–21

> 1:19 **You must understand this, my beloved: let everyone be quick to listen, slow to speak, slow to anger;** [20] **for your anger does not produce God's righteousness.** [21] **Therefore rid yourselves of all sordidness and rank growth of wickedness, and welcome with meekness the implanted word that has the power to save your souls.**

This section of James opens with a threefold appeal: "Let everyone be quick to listen, slow to speak, slow to anger." James values listening, temperate speech, and humility in all areas of life. In particular, however, we are urged to "be quick to listen, slow to speak, slow to anger" as we come before the "word of truth" (v. 18)—"the implanted word" that has the power to save our lives (v. 21). That word is none other than the word of the gospel, that is, God's word to us of mercy, power, and renewal in Jesus Christ. One of our primary and ongoing tasks as Christians is to attend to that word as it comes to us in preaching and the sacraments, in teaching, in tradition, and in careful study of the scriptures. It is an urgent task ("be *quick* to listen"), and where Christians are thus engaged they will be "slow to speak." They must listen carefully and patiently to God before they presume to speak and act in God's name.

Moreover, James urges Christians to "rid themselves" of anything that hinders reception of God's word. James refers to the gospel as an "implanted word," for just as the sower in Jesus' parable faithfully sows the word (Mark 4), so has the word, through the preaching and teaching of many faithful witnesses, been implanted in our lives. It is James's hope that we will come to the word with openness and, through careful attention to it, nurture its growth in our lives.

DOING THE WORD
James 1:22–25

1:22 **But be doers of the word, and not merely hearers who deceive themselves.** [23] **For if any are hearers of the word and not doers, they are like those who look at themselves in a mirror;** [24] **for they look at themselves and, on going away, immediately forget what they were like.** [25] **But those who look into the perfect law, the law of liberty, and persevere, being not hearers who forget but doers who act—they will be blessed in their doing.**

In James's view, the faithful hearing of the word leads to the doing of it, for receptive hearing involves commitment and obedience to what has been heard. It is important to note that James does not contrast hearers and doers, but rather compares two kinds of hearers: those who act upon what they have heard and those who do not. "Hearers" always precedes "doing" and is the foundation for it. Hearers directs and empowers our response to God's word. Nevertheless, once we have received the implanted word and have been renewed, directed, and empowered by it, we are expected to bloom.

To make this point, James draws on a striking, though puzzling, illustration. Those who are hearers of the word, but not doers, are compared to "those who look at themselves in a mirror" then immediately forget their image once they have stepped away. Perhaps James's point is that they look into the mirror and see that changes in their appearance are called for, but they fail to make the necessary alterations—they step away with hair still unkempt and clothes askew. Or perhaps he thinks that they look into the mirror and see grace and forgiveness reflected there, but the impression is only fleeting, and they step away from the newness of life that has been wrought by the word. Whichever the case, hearing that does not lead to doing is worthless. Those who come before God's word in this manner are deceiving themselves if they think that they have really heard (v. 22).

These "hearers who forget" are contrasted with those who hear the word, attend to it, persevere in it, and act upon it—those who translate the implications of the gospel into their lives. The word is referred to as "law" (v. 25), because once received, it implies commitment and obedience. Moreover, the "law" to which James refers is none other than the will of God for our lives as revealed in the Old Testament and in the life and teaching of Jesus Christ. That will, or "law," is "perfect" because it is complete, lacking in nothing (compare 1:4), and because it leads therefore to the "perfection" or "maturity" or "wholeness" that is James's hope for Christian life. It is also referred to as a "law of liberty," because it liberates us from false slaveries and desires (1:14 –15) and has the power to save our souls (v. 21).

Cosmetics magnate Esteé Lauder insists that "a good mirror is the most important accessory in a woman's life." She is right, but for reasons other than she supposes! All of us—women and men—need a good mirror that will help us see ourselves as we really are. James reminds us that there is only one mirror that shows forth our true reflection: the gospel of Jesus Christ. In that mirror, which James holds before us, we see who we are in the light of God's love and what we are meant to be.

GENUINE RELIGION
James 1:26–27

> 1:26 **If any think they are religious, and do not bridle their tongues but deceive their hearts, their religion is worthless.** 27 **Religion that is pure and undefiled before God, the Father, is this: to care for orphans and widows in their distress, and to keep oneself unstained by the world.**

In James's view, genuinely religious persons are "doers of the word, and not hearers only." But of what does authentic religious activity consist? James makes three concrete suggestions. First, right hearing of God's word is never without effect on our speaking—on what we say and how we speak to one another. Indeed, James suggests that "if any think they are religious, and do not bridle their tongues but deceive their hearts, their religion is worthless." Right hearing of the word empowers us for self-control and, in James's view, nowhere is self-control more urgently needed than in our speaking (see James 3).

Second, genuine religion consists of caring "for orphans and widows in their distress." In so advising, James stands squarely in the tradition of the

Hebrew scriptures, in which widows and orphans are frequently lifted up as representative of the oppressed and as a special focus of God's concern (see Isa. 1:16–17). For James, too, they are representative of all who find themselves defenseless and suffering poverty, distress, and oppression. Genuine religion is marked by care and concern for people in need.

Finally, genuine religion consists of keeping oneself "unstained by the world." In so advising, James by no means suggests that Christians are to refrain from involvement in the world. Has it not just commended attention to those in need? Rather, the author encourages Christians to take full part in the affairs of the world but not to embrace the world's standards. James uses the term *world* to refer to ways of thinking and systems of values that do not take God's existence and God's claims into account (Johnson, "Friendship," 173–74). Christians are to be engaged in the world, but they are to hold a different understanding of reality and a different set of values, informed by their experience of the grace of God in Jesus Christ.

The same viewpoint is reflected in the words of Jesus in John's Gospel, where he speaks of Christians as being "in the world" but "not of the world" (John 17:14–18). Similarly, the apostle Paul urges us Christians not to be "conformed to this world" but to be "transformed" by the renewing of our minds, that we may "discern what is the will of God—what is good and acceptable and perfect" (Rom. 12:2).

Religion, then, is a great deal more than doctrine or rituals, although it includes these. In the final analysis—for James at least—the test of genuine religion is not orthodoxy (right belief) but orthopraxy (right practice).

13. Beware of Discrimination
James 2:1–13

In 2:1–13, James tackles head-on the problem of discrimination in the Christian community. In James's view, "acts of favoritism" are inconsistent with Christian faith.

WARNING AGAINST DISCRIMINATION
James 2:1–4

> 2:1 **My brothers and sisters, do you with your acts of favoritism really believe in our glorious Lord Jesus Christ?** [2] **For if a person with gold rings and in fine clothes comes into your assembly, and if a poor person in dirty clothes also comes in,** [3] **and if you take notice of the one wearing the fine clothes and say, "Have a seat here, please," while to the one who is poor you say, "Stand there," or, "Sit at my feet,"** [4] **have you not made distinctions among yourselves, and become judges with evil thoughts?**

James maintains that faith in Jesus Christ bears directly upon our treatment of persons. Thus signs of snobbery and partiality in the Christian community prompt an incredulous question: "My brothers and sisters, do you with your acts of favoritism really believe in our glorious Lord Jesus Christ?"

The fact that James refers to "*acts* of favoritism" in the plural form suggests that discrimination can manifest itself in the Christian community in a variety of ways. But by using a flagrant example, the author leaves no doubt as to the kind of attitude and behavior deemed incompatible with Christian faith. Two visitors are depicted as entering the Christian assembly: one bejeweled and one bedraggled; one from the lap of luxury and the other, perhaps, from the streets. The extreme contrast in their appearance is highlighted: The bejeweled visitor is dressed in "fine clothes" and the poor visitor in "dirty clothes."

These sharply contrasted people are given correspondingly contrasting receptions. The bejeweled visitor is treated with extreme courtesy ("Have a seat here, please"), while the bedraggled guest is brusquely shuffled aside ("Stand there" or "Sit at my feet"). When Christians "make distinctions" among themselves in any such manner, haven't they "become judges with evil thoughts"? (See Lev. 19:15.) Are they not manifesting that internal dividedness that belies integrity of faith? By kowtowing to the counterfeit glory of the splendidly attired, have they not betrayed the truly glorious one who alone is to be exalted in the Christian community and before whom all are equal: "our glorious Lord Jesus Christ" (2:1)?

WHY DISCRIMINATION IS INCONSISTENT WITH CHRISTIAN FAITH
James 2:5–13

2:5 **Listen, my beloved brothers and sisters. Has not God chosen the poor in the world to be rich in faith and to be heirs of the kingdom that he has promised to those who love him?** 6 **But you have dishonored the poor. Is it not the rich who oppress you? Is it not they who drag you into court?** 7 **Is it not they who blaspheme the excellent name that was invoked over you?**

8 **You do well if you really fulfill the royal law according to the scripture, "You shall love your neighbor as yourself."** 9 **But if you show partiality, you commit sin and are convicted by the law as transgressors.** 10 **For whoever keeps the whole law but fails in one point has become accountable for all of it.** 11 **For the one who said, "You shall not commit adultery," also said, "You shall not murder." Now if you do not commit adultery but if you murder, you have become a transgressor of the law.** 12 **So speak and so act as those who are to be judged by the law of liberty.** 13 **For judgment will be without mercy to anyone who has shown no mercy; mercy triumphs over judgment.**

To James's way of thinking, the kind of snobbery depicted in verses 2–4 is far from a trivial matter. In fact, the author proceeds to establish three grounds on which acts of favoritism constitute a serious denial of faith. First, he reminds his readers of God's special care and concern for the poor (v. 5)—a concern that is stressed throughout the scriptures (see Luke 6:20). It should be clear, then, that when members of the Christian community ignore the poor, they are not reflecting God's compassion. When they slight the poor, they dishonor those whom God has honored, whom God has "chosen" to be "rich in faith" and "heirs of the kingdom." How is it that the prejudices of the world rather than the preferences of God come to be manifested in a community of God's people?

Second, the author appeals to his readers' own experiences. He suggests that acts of favoritism make little sense in light of the way they themselves are treated at the hands of the rich: "Is it not the rich who oppress you? Is it not they who drag you into court? Is it not they who blaspheme the excellent name that was invoked over you?"

James's letter reflects a time when persons of wealth were not yet often found in the church—at least not in the communities with which the author was most closely associated. Members of the Christian community may very well have been taken to court by the rich over such issues as debts, rents, and wages (see 5:4–6). As a result, they may also have found themselves the objects of slander and popular gossip on the part of the rich—disparaged as bad citizens or unreliable debtors. James regards any such treatment as blasphemy, for Christians bear the name of Jesus from the moment they are baptized in the name of Christ (see Acts 2:38). In James's view, abuse of those who bear the name of Christ is abuse of Christ himself. Thus it is bewildering that members of the Christian community should grovel before those who exploit the poor, harass Christians, and dishonor Christ.

Third, the author insists that partiality toward the rich is also a transgression of the biblical principle of love. Readers are reminded of the familiar commandment to "love your neighbor as yourself" (Lev. 19:18). This commandment, in fact, is referred to as the "royal law," because it is the law of the kingdom into which God has called them (see Mark 12:29–31).

Those whom James addresses may very well have argued, as do we, that in attending to the rich they are showing love to their neighbors. And if this is really the case, then they "do well." But this is no excuse for partiality. If in attending to the rich, readers discriminate against the poor, then they "commit sin and are convicted by the law as transgressors" (v. 9). They have not understood that the poor person whom they dishonor is also a neighbor and that "acts of favoritism" place them in violation of the biblical commandment to love.

Moreover, "acts of favoritism" are not to be dismissed as minor infractions of God's command—as misdemeanors rather than felonies. In order to underline the seriousness of the crime of partiality, James draws on the ancient Jewish doctrine of the complete unity of the law and contends that to violate the law at this one point is to break the law as a whole (v. 10; compare Gal. 5:3). To illustrate this point, James links partiality with the heinous sins of adultery and murder—sins readers would not fail to consider serious. Adulterers will not suppose that they should be excused of adultery because they have not committed murder (v. 11). James's point is that the adulterer stands guilty before the law, as does the murderer—and as does the one who discriminates. God, who forbids adultery and murder, also forbids discrimination. God stands behind *every* commandment. Thus, all three—the adulterer, the murderer, and the one who commits "acts of favoritism"—are transgressors of the law and are subject to God's judgment.

In closing, James reminds us all that we are accountable to God for our words and deeds (v. 12). At the last day, every individual will stand before the judgment seat of God. What will be determined at that point is not whether we are to be "saved"; we have already been saved by the grace of God through faith in Jesus Christ. What the judgment will reveal is whether or not we have misused the grace that is ours—whether or not we have embodied in our lives the possibilities the gospel offers. Our practice of indiscriminate love toward all people will reveal whether we have allowed the grace and power of God to produce a transformation in our lives. Impartiality in all our doings is, in no small part, a sign of the integrity of faith.

Clearly, James has much to contribute to our thinking about acts and experiences of discrimination. Indeed, Howard University scholar Cain Hope Felder observes that James 2:1–13 provides what is perhaps the strongest castigation of class discrimination in the New Testament—or for that matter, any discrimination based on outward appearance—and that these words have particular pertinence for African Americans who still experience such discrimination daily (*Troubling Biblical Waters*, 118–19).

The fact that James speaks of "acts of favoritism" (plural!) should prompt us to ponder *all* those experiences in which we have made snap judgments about others on the basis of outward appearance—perhaps on the basis of disability, dress, race, class, gender, or age. From James's perspective, discrimination of any kind is simply inconsistent with Christian faith.

14. Faith and Works
James 2:14–26

2:14 **What good is it, my brothers and sisters, if you say you have faith, but do not have works? Can faith save you?** [15] **If a brother or sister is naked and lacks daily food,** [16] **and one of you says to them, "Go in peace; keep warm and eat your fill," and yet you do not supply their bodily needs, what is the good of that?** [17] **So faith by itself, if it has no works, is dead.**

[18] **But someone will say, "You have faith and I have works." Show me your faith apart from your works, and I by my works will show you my faith.** [19] **You believe that God is one; you do well. Even the demons believe—and shudder.** [20] **Do you want to be shown, you senseless person, that faith apart from works is barren?** [21] **Was not our ancestor Abraham justified by works when he offered his son Isaac on the altar?** [22] **You see that faith was active along with his works, and faith was brought to completion by the works.** [23] **Thus the scripture was fulfilled that says, "Abraham believed God, and it was reckoned to him as righteousness," and he was called the friend of God.** [24] **You see that a person is justified by works and not by faith alone.** [25] **Likewise, was not Rahab the prostitute also justified by works when she welcomed the messengers and sent them out by another road?** [26] **For just as the body without the spirit is dead, so faith without works is also dead.**

James is best known for its insistence on the inseparable connection between faith and works. This theme, which finds its clearest expression in 2:14–26, undergirds all the ethical exhortation in the letter. Whether James speaks of ministering to orphans and widows, meeting the needs of the poor, resisting discrimination, or controlling the tongue, it speaks of "works"—works that are intrinsically related to faith and are its proper expression.

But if this is the theme for which James is best known, it is also the one that is most problematic. Indeed, we have arrived at the most controversial and misunderstood part of the whole letter. This section of James, more than anything else, prompted Martin Luther to say "I almost feel like throwing Jimmy into the stove." Luther was concerned, as others too have been, that James seems to contradict a central biblical affirmation—that of justification by grace through faith alone. We will inquire as to whether James is guilty as charged!

DOES JAMES CONTRADICT PAUL?

James has been accused frequently of standing in direct contradiction to the apostle Paul and to the very heart of Christian faith. In Romans 3:28, Paul states quite emphatically that "we hold that a person is justified by faith apart from works prescribed by the law." Indeed, Paul's affirmation that we are brought into right relationship with God by God's grace alone and not by meritorious works, sparked the Protestant Reformation in the sixteenth century and is central to both Protestant and modern Roman Catholic faith.

Thus when the author of James insists that "a person is justified by works and not by faith alone" (2:24), is he not proposing a new way of salvation? Is he not distorting the very heart of Christian faith? Before jumping to this conclusion, it is important to take note of the fact that Paul and James are addressing different struggles, and each intend quite different things by "works."

Paul, on the one hand, addresses the starting point of faith—the question of how one is brought into right relationship with God. He battles the notion that one must perform meritorious works to earn God's acceptance and approval. The works to which he refers are "works of the law" and include such matters as compliance with food laws, circumcision, purification rites, and ritual prescriptions. None of these matters, Paul argues, are requirements for salvation, for salvation is a gracious gift of God, to be accepted by faith alone, apart from any such works of the law.

The letter of James, on the other hand, does not address the initial experience of acceptance by God, but the continuing life of the believer. It does not speak of "works" as meritorious deeds aimed to win God's approval, but rather as the fruit of Christian faith (see also Matt. 12:33). Moreover, when James speaks of "works," it refers not to "works of the law" such as legal observances, but rather to acts of love in the neighbor's behalf. Therefore, works, for James, include such matters as the care of widows and orphans, respect for the poor, feeding the hungry, clothing the naked, and control of the tongue. From James's viewpoint, genuine faith cannot exist without producing this kind of works as the fruit of obedience.

It is also important to note that James insists upon the inseparability of faith and works throughout the discussion in 2:14–26. At no point does James contrast faith and works. Instead, the contrast is between two kinds of faith: genuine faith (of which works are a sign) and counterfeit faith (which finds no expression in works and thus cannot really be "faith" at all). Faith, when it is genuine, is inseparable from works, which are its proper expression. Therefore, in 2:14, the question is not "What good is it if you have faith but do not have works?" but rather "What good is it if you *say* you have faith but do not have works?"

To James's way of thinking, faith that fails to issue in works is not deserving of the name "faith" at all. Thus when we read that "a person is justified by works and not by faith alone," we must bear in mind that James speaks of works that are grounded in faith and are the proper expression of it. And James speaks of "faith alone" as counterfeit faith, because it does not produce the fruit of faith. Works by themselves are not saving; they are saving only because they manifest genuine faith.

Another important difference between Paul and James is that when Paul speaks of "justification," his eyes are focused, as we have noted, on the starting point of the Christian life. However, when the author of James speaks of "justification," his eyes are focused on the final judgment. He speaks of "justification" in connection with the last day, when it will be determined whether believers have embodied in their lives the possibilities the gospel offers (see Matt. 25:31–46; and the emphasis on final judgment in James 2:12; 3:1; 5:1–6, 7–9).

The distinguished preacher Ernest Campbell captures the difference between Paul and James with a helpful analogy: Paul is dealing with obstetrics, with how new life begins; James, however, is dealing with pediatrics and geriatrics, with how Christian life grows and matures and ages ("Toward a Protestant Doctrine of Works")!

Thus, while their emphases differ, Paul and James do not stand as directly in opposition to each other as they might appear to at first glance. In fact, most interpreters agree that James is not responding directly to Paul at all but rather to an area of the church in which Paul's *slogan* of "justification by faith" was being used and distorted to argue that "faith alone" was all that counted, without any accompanying moral fruit or transformation of life.

Moreover, both Paul and James are needed to keep Christian faith in perspective. Paul forcefully reminds us that there is nothing we can do to "earn" God's grace and forgiveness. We can only accept it. This affirmation bears constant repeating, lest we fall into the trap of "works righteousness"—of thinking that we must earn God's grace and approval with good works.

James, however, forcefully reminds us that works are intrinsically related to faith and are, in fact, its proper expression. This affirmation also bears repeating, lest we proclaim "cheap grace"—that is, lest we forget that Christians are called to be disciples and that genuine faith finds expression in a lifestyle that is compatible with one's convictions. God's grace comes to us as mercy, and also as power for transformation of our lives!

ILLUSTRATIONS OF THE INSEPARABILITY OF FAITH AND WORKS

Within 2:14–26, a number of illustrations bear witness to the inseparability of faith and works. First, James offers a hypothetical example: "If a brother or sister is naked and lacks daily food, and one of you says to them, 'Go in peace; keep warm and eat your fill,' and yet you do not supply their bodily needs, what is the good of that?" It is no accident that the example entails neglect of the poor, for the author would especially like to see "works" done by Christians on behalf of the poor.

Martin Luther King, Jr. echoed James's viewpoint when he suggested in *Stride Toward Freedom: The Montgomery Story* that any religion that professes concern for people's souls and is not concerned with the economic and social conditions that oppress them is a "dry-as-dust religion." Or as James so bluntly puts it, "faith by itself, if it has no works, is dead."

James argues further, using a humorous illustration in 2:19: "You believe that God is one; you do well. Even the demons believe—and shudder." James lifts up a central confession shared by both Jews and Christians (see Deut. 6:4–9) and acknowledges that this is an orthodox belief—correct theological opinion. Then he makes a telling observation: The demons are quite orthodox! They too believe that there is one God alone, but they shudder in fear of the judgment day. The point is that faith is more than orthodox belief. Genuine, saving faith is enacted in works, which are its proper expression.

To this negative example of "faith without works," James then adds two positive scriptural examples of faith in action. First, James points to Abraham, the Old Testament patriarch whose faith was demonstrated in his willingness to offer his son Isaac as a sacrifice in obedience to God's will

(Genesis 22). Second, James points to the example of Rahab the prostitute, whose faith in Israel's God moved her to protect Israelite spies when they arrived in Jericho (Josh. 2:1–21).

Finally, an apt analogy in 2:26 summarizes James's point. The word "spirit" can also mean "breath," and this is probably James's intention. Just as breathing is a sign that the body is alive, so are works a sign that faith is alive. When the body is without breath, it is a corpse. So faith without works is also dead!

15. Taming the Tongue
James 3:1–12

"Sticks and stones may break my bones, but words can never hurt me"—or so the saying goes. But who has not been wounded by words? And who has not been tormented by the painful memory of words we wish we had never said? James knows that words can hurt. Indeed, a large section of this short letter is devoted to the dangers of the tongue. In James's view, disciplined speech should be of utmost concern to Christians.

THE POWER OF THE TONGUE
James 3:1–5a

> 3:1 **Not many of you should become teachers, my brothers and sisters, for you know that we who teach will be judged with greater strictness.** [2] **For all of us make many mistakes. Anyone who makes no mistakes in speaking is perfect, able to keep the whole body in check with a bridle.** [3] **If we put bits into the mouths of horses to make them obey us, we guide their whole bodies.** [4] **Or look at ships: though they are so large that it takes strong winds to drive them, yet they are guided by a very small rudder wherever the will of the pilot directs.** [5] **So also the tongue is a small member, yet it boasts of great exploits.**

James's counsel on the tongue opens with a word of warning to would-be teachers: "Not many of you should become teachers, my brothers and sisters, for you know that we who teach will be judged with greater strictness." The reason for this warning becomes plain as the author zeroes in on his central point of interest. While all people make mistakes, teachers are at special risk, for the tongue, the teacher's chief tool of trade, is a powerful and dangerous instrument. But all believers are implied in this dramatic portrait of the tongue.

Of all the sins by which people stumble, those of the tongue are the most difficult to avoid. Indeed, James holds forth the ideal of the "perfect" person as one who makes no mistakes in what he or she says and is therefore "able to keep the whole body in check with a bridle." ("Perfection" refers not to "sinlessness" but to the "maturity," the "wholeness," the "integrity" of Christian life; see 1:4). James may be suggesting that those who are able to control the tongue can certainly do that which is far easier, which is to control the body also. Or James may be suggesting that by controlling one's words, one thereby gains control of the body as a whole. Sinful deeds and impulses are often dependent upon the igniting spark of the tongue.

Whichever of these suggestions is intended, the thought leads to a series of dramatic images that highlight the importance of disciplined speech. The images illustrate the astonishing potential of the tongue, which exercises a power and influence far out of proportion to its small size. Like the bit in the mouth of a horse, or like the rudder guiding a wind-tossed ship, the tongue also is small in size but great in its effect. In sum, "the tongue is a small member, yet it boasts of great exploits." The boast is not challenged, for James is keenly aware of the awesome power of speech.

THE TONGUE'S
POTENTIAL FOR EVIL
James 3:5b–8

> 3:5b **How great a forest is set ablaze by a small fire!** [6] **And the tongue is a fire. The tongue is placed among our members as a world of iniquity; it stains the whole body, sets on fire the cycle of nature, and is itself set on fire by hell.** [7] **For every species of beast and bird, of reptile and sea creature, can be tamed and has been tamed by the human species,** [8] **but no one can tame the tongue—a restless evil, full of deadly poison.**

The great power of the tongue can also be used for evil purposes. This potential is clearly at the heart of James's concern, for a spiraling series of remarkable images now graphically portray the destructive effect of undisciplined speech.

The tongue is likened to a fire, which, though small, is capable of wild and far-reaching devastation: "How great a forest is set ablaze by a small fire!" Moreover, it sets on fire the "cycle of nature"—a peculiar phrase with which James appears to suggest that the tongue's devastating effect is felt throughout the entire course of human life, from the cradle to the grave. And no one can tame it!

James underscores the inability of humans to discipline their speech. Although human beings, who have been given dominion over the earth (Genesis 1), exercise mastery over the whole animal world, they cannot master their own unruly tongues. The tongue alone is beyond control. Indeed, it is "a restless evil, full of deadly poison," akin to the venomous tongue of a snake. The imagery is severe and exaggerated to be sure—the better to impress upon us the dangerous potential of uncontrolled speech.

THE INCONSISTENCY OF THE TONGUE
James 3:9–12

> 3:9 **With it we bless the Lord and Father, and with it we curse those who are made in the likeness of God.** [10] **From the same mouth come blessing and cursing. My brothers and sisters, this ought not to be so.** [11] **Does a spring pour forth from the same opening both fresh and brackish water?** [12] **Can a fig tree, my brothers and sisters, yield olives, or a grapevine figs? No more can salt water yield fresh.**

James motivates us to make every effort to tame the tongue. Thus it censures the inconsistency of uncontrolled speech. The tongue is fickle, and to illustrate this point James provides a specific example of inconsistent speech: "With it we bless the Lord and Father, and with it we curse those who are made in the likeness of God. From the same mouth come blessing and cursing" (vv. 9–10). It is not right that the tongue be used for such incompatible activities, that it should bless God and curse human beings who have been created by God in the divine image. Such inconsistent speech is indicative of the double-mindedness condemned in 1:8 and 4:8 and is utterly inappropriate for believers.

James rests this case with an appeal to the world of nature, highlighting with a final series of images the absurdity of inconsistent speech. Such speech should be as much out of the question for the believer as it would be for a spring to yield both fresh water and brackish, or for a fig tree to produce olives. Nature is not guilty of the duplicity that characterizes the human tongue.

These final images call us to restore integrity and discipline to Christian speech. Change is possible, in James's view, or else so much energy would not have been expended on this topic of disciplined speech. To be sure, change will not be accomplished through our own efforts alone (3:8) but in reliance upon the power of God "who gives to all generously and ungrudgingly" that we may be "mature and complete" (1:4–5).

James's reflection on the tongue may be among the most perennially relevant words in the whole letter. It bears on present-day Christian life on a variety of fronts. In recent years, for example, many Christians have become increasingly aware of the ways in which the tongue can "exclude," that is, to the ways in which the words we use can consciously or unconsciously give expression to sexism, racism, and other prejudices. Thus many Christians have committed themselves to the use of "inclusive language," for it is not a trivial matter: It addresses the question of who is included in God's grace and bears as well on our imaging and understanding of God's presence in our lives. Interestingly, James is a model of disciplined, inclusive speech, for the letter balances male and female imagery in a manner quite unique in the New Testament (see 1:17–18; 2:15, 21–25).

In the church and in our society at large, we are also becoming increasingly conscious of the power of words to disempower and humiliate. While attention to this matter centers on appropriate speech between men and women, it also bears on the manner in which parents and children, husbands and wives, and teachers and students speak to each other. Moreover, "gossip" is a constant theme of community life. Thus an oft-repeated remark gives expression to what is often our community spirit: "If you can't say something good about someone, come over here and sit next to me."

It is important for Christians to talk with and about each other in order that they may know and care for each other. After all, Christians are members of a family by virtue of baptism and should aspire to be the sort of people who know a great deal about one another without using that information to hurt one another. Reflection on James may help us turn our tongues to constructive rather than destructive ends.

Finally, in connection with James's discussion, it is important to remember that the tongue's potential for evil can also include silence. Sometimes failure to speak—failure to use our tongues—can damage our family, church, or community (local, national, international) relationships. Thus we should note that James does not counsel us to "zipper" the tongue. Instead we are urged to "bridle" it (1:26; 3:2). The bridle does not stop the horse from running; it helps the horse run in a more disciplined direction. This is James's hope for Christian speech.

16. Friendship with God
James 3:13–4:12

Throughout James, the "double-minded person" has been continually before us: the person who looks both to the world and to God for values and security and so compromises his or her integrity of faith; the person prone to double-talk, double-face, double-vision. Double-mindedness may be a particular peril to Christians who live in a cultural context where it is often assumed that the values of God and the values of their society are one and the same. In 3:13–4:12, however, James reminds us that what God values and what the world values are quite dissimilar. Indeed, James directly challenges those who are double-minded to get off the fence! Two lifestyles are set squarely before us and we are asked to choose.

TWO KINDS OF WISDOM
James 3:13–18

> 3:13 **Who is wise and understanding among you? Show by your good life that your works are done with gentleness born of wisdom.** [14] **But if you have bitter envy and selfish ambition in your hearts, do not be boastful and false to the truth.** [15] **Such wisdom does not come from above, but is earthly, unspiritual, devilish.** [16] **For where there is envy and selfish ambition, there will also be disorder and wickedness of every kind.** [17] **But the wisdom from above is first pure, then peaceable, gentle, willing to yield, full of mercy and good fruits, without a trace of partiality or hypocrisy.** [18] **And a harvest of righteousness is sown in peace for those who make peace.**

The challenge to fence-sitters is presented by means of two pointed contrasts. The first is a contrast between two kinds of wisdom: a true wisdom that "comes down from above" and a pseudowisdom that is "earthly, unspiritual, devilish." The true wisdom of which James speaks has little to do with intellectual brilliance. It is not a wisdom that is achieved by going to school. As stated in 1:5, it is entirely a gift of God, "who gives to all generously and ungrudgingly." This wisdom consists of knowledge of how to live according to God's ways. Thus the truly "wise and understanding" person manifests his or her wisdom not by superior arguments or brilliance of mind, but by a "good life"—by "works" that "are done with gentleness born of wisdom." Once again James declares that actions speak louder than words! True wisdom is manifested in one's conduct—in a manner of life that is, above all, peaceable.

According to James, quarrelsome behavior belies any claim to true wisdom. True wisdom leads to peaceable conduct, not to jealousy or selfish ambition, desires which destroy the fabric of human community. Divisive behaviors are inspired by a malevolent sort of "wisdom," a false wisdom that is "earthly, unspiritual, devilish"—that is, the sort of wisdom that a demon might possess! For just as the demon's "faith" (2:19) fails to manifest itself in works that are faith's proper expression, so too does earthly, unspiritual, demonic "wisdom" fail to manifest itself in deeds of righteousness and peacemaking.

FRIENDSHIP WITH THE WORLD OR FRIENDSHIP WITH GOD?
James 4:1–6

4:1 Those conflicts and disputes among you, where do they come from? Do they not come from your cravings that are at war within you? 2 You want something and do not have it; so you commit murder. And you covet something and cannot obtain it; so you engage in disputes and conflicts. You do not have, because you do not ask. 3 You ask and do not receive, because you ask wrongly, in order to spend what you get on your pleasures. 4 Adulterers! Do you not know that friendship with the world is enmity with God? Therefore whoever wishes to be a friend of the world becomes an enemy of God. 5 Or do you suppose that it is for nothing that the scripture says, "God yearns jealously for the spirit that he has made to dwell in us"? 6 But he gives all the more grace; therefore it says,
    "God opposes the proud, but gives grace to the humble."

The second contrast is stated even more sharply. Fence-sitters are challenged to choose between two alternatives: friendship with the world or friendship with God. James has already suggested in 1:27 that genuine religion consists of keeping oneself "unstained by the world." This does not mean that Christians are to refrain from taking part in the world's affairs, as we noted earlier, but that they should not embrace the world's standards. The term *world* refers to ways of thinking and systems of values that do not take God's existence and God's claims into account. Christians are to be engaged in the world, but with a different understanding of reality and a different set of values, informed by the experience of the grace of God in Jesus Christ.

In 4:1–4, James further unmasks the worldly disposition: It is one that places self and the pursuit of pleasure at the center of one's aspirations and activities. As a result, it tends toward a life that is largely destructive of persons. Self-centered enviousness leads to covetousness, disputes, conflicts, and even murder. Moreover, it is a disposition that leads one to forego prayer, or to use prayer as one more means to gratify desires.

"Envy" and "covetousness" are emphasized repeatedly in 3:13–4:6 for, in James's view, they are at the heart of all human conflict and a central mark of friendship with the world and of wisdom from below. And are not envy and covetousness in fact often the enemy of personal peace, peace in the family, peace in the church, peace in the nation, and peace in the world?

James's indictment issues in a harsh rebuke: "Adulterers!" James draws on a familiar biblical imagery, which compares the relationship between God and the chosen people as a marriage, when he gives this rebuke to the "unfaithful partner": "Do you not know that friendship with the world is enmity with God?" The rich imagery of a marriage gives expression to the exclusive commitment and devotion demanded of God's people.

James also draws on the language of friendship. For James, friendship has a special meaning. As I noted earlier (see page 84), friendship was not a casual affection in the first-century world. It was a much discussed and highly esteemed relationship. Indeed, friends were considered "one soul," which meant "at the least, to share the same attitudes and values and perceptions, to see things the same way" (Johnson, "Friendship," 173).

One must choose between friendship with the world and friendship with God, for it is not possible to share the attitudes, values, and perceptions of both God and the world simultaneously! A double-minded person wishes to be a friend of both! These two ways of life are simply incompatible; they are mutually exclusive. Indeed, James states that "whoever wishes to be a friend of the world becomes an *enemy* of God."

Double-mindedness grieves our rejected partner and friend, as well as evokes divine jealously. God yearns for our single-minded devotion and desires for our return. James reminds us in verse 6 that we may return to God in humble repentance, and the relationship will be graciously restored.

CALL TO REPENTANCE
James 4:7–12

> 4:7 **Submit yourselves therefore to God. Resist the devil, and he will flee from you.** [8] **Draw near to God, and he will draw near to you. Cleanse your hands, you sinners, and purify your hearts, you double-minded.** [9] **Lament and mourn and weep. Let your laughter be turned into mourning and your joy into dejection.** [10] **Humble yourselves before the Lord, and he will exalt you.**
>
> [11] **Do not speak evil against one another, brothers and sisters. Whoever speaks evil against another or judges another, speaks evil against the law and judges the law; but if you judge the law, you are not a doer of the law but a judge.** [12] **There is one lawgiver and judge who is able to save and to destroy. So who, then, are you to judge your neighbor?**

Two distinct ways of life, then, lie before Christians, and we are challenged to choose which one we will embrace. We can embrace "wisdom from below" and "friendship with the world" and exist as if God has no claim on our lives, if we so choose. However, God has made available another way of life. Through the gift of the gospel—the "implanted word"—in our lives (1:21), through the gift of God's "wisdom from above," we have been empowered to embrace God's own intentions for human life.

Having sharply stated the two incompatible options before us, James calls for a radical decision on our part. We are called away from uncommitted double-mindedness to single-minded devotion to God. We are called to terminate our affair with the world and to renew our friendship with God. These concluding verses constitute, in effect, a call to radical repentance. That call is accompanied by reassurance that God's response will be one of expansive graciousness. Right relationship to God, however, also bears on our relationship to others. Thus, in the final verses, James addresses the necessity for right relationships among fellow Christians.

Perhaps it is good to remind ourselves that the letter is addressed to people who have already heard the gospel, to people who have already been made friends of God through Jesus Christ! This passage reminds us that our friendship with God, like all friendships, is a living reality and must continually be nourished and renewed. Living the Christian life entails continual recommitment to sharing the attitudes, values, and perceptions of God—to embodying God's own intentions for human life.

17. Wealth and Poverty
James 4:13–5:6

James speaks vigorously and repeatedly about economic realities (1:9–11, 27; 2:1–7, 15–16; 4:13–5:6). Its discussion of this matter is not easy reading—for many North American Christians at least. Indeed, the novelist Upton Sinclair once read some of James's thoughts on this subject to a crowd of clerygmen and suggested that the words came from a woman terrorist agitator. The ministers were furious at the nerve of the novelist and declared that the rebel ought to be deported. The words read on that occasion are now before us—James's most pointed words on wealth and poverty.

FAITH AND BUSINESS PRACTICE
James 4:13–17

> 4:13 **Come now, you who say, "Today or tomorrow we will go to such and such a town and spend a year there, doing business and making money."** [14] **Yet you do not even know what tomorrow will bring. What is your life? For you are a mist that appears for a little while and then vanishes.** [15] **Instead you ought to say, "If the Lord wishes, we will live and do this or that."** [16] **As it is, you boast in your arrogance; all such boasting is evil.** [17] **Anyone, then, who knows the right thing to do and fails to do it, commits sin.**

The letter of James insists that faith transforms routine pursuits into arenas for discipleship. Business practices are not excluded. Indeed James sharply chastises any who neglect God's sovereignty over commercial endeavors.

"Come now, you who say, 'Today or tomorrow we will go to such and such a town and spend a year there, doing business and making money' " (v. 13). James does not chastise business practices as such. It does not condemn intelligent planning for the future. What is rebuked is the arrogant assumption that life consists of doing business and making money, that human calculation can secure the future. James mocks any such arrogance by forcefully reminding us that all our projects—indeed our very lives—are provisional. Life is uncertain and transitory. The future is not in our control, and we do not know what it will bring. In everything, we are utterly dependent upon the living God.

Thus, instead of assuming that we are self-sufficient or that we control our destiny, we should acknowledge our dependence upon God. We ought to say that "If the Lord wishes, we will live and do this or that." In fact, the familiar expression, "God willing," is attributed to James. We are to commit our plans to the will of God.

Moreover, we are to apply our faith to our business practices. God is sovereign over all of life, and our business pursuits, like all the activities of our lives, are to be informed and transformed by God's presence, power, and intentions—or else we are liable to sin.

Indeed we sin not only by doing what is wrong. "Anyone who knows the right thing to do and fails to do it, commits sin" as well. Thus we are encouraged to embody God's intentions for human life in our business practices and in all our endeavors.

DENUNCIATION OF THE RICH
James 5:1–6

> 5:1 **Come now, you rich people, weep and wail for the miseries that are coming to you.** [2] **Your riches have rotted, and your clothes are moth-eaten.** [3] **Your gold and silver have rusted, and their rust will be evidence against you, and it will eat your flesh like fire. You have laid up treasure for the last days.** [4] **Listen! The wages of the laborers who mowed your fields, which you kept back by fraud, cry out, and the cries of the harvesters have reached the ears of the Lord of hosts.** [5] **You have lived on the earth in luxury and in pleasure; you have fattened your hearts in a day of slaughter.** [6] **You have condemned and murdered the righteous one, who does not resist you.**

We have had reason to suspect that the author of James is not positively inclined toward the rich (1:9–11; 2:6–7)! But now there may be no doubt about his animosity, for he unleashes his fury in fierce denunciations. The rich are invited to "weep and wail" for the miseries that are coming upon them, and in harsh, graphic language reminiscent of the Old Testament prophets, James announces the disasters that surely await them on the judgment day.

The rich are warned of the loss of their possessions: "Your riches have rotted, and your clothes are moth-eaten. Your gold and silver have rusted." Moreover, "their rust will be evidence against" them, testifying to the fact that it has lain idle and has not been used to benefit others.

Two specific charges are then leveled against the rich. First, James declares them guilty of oppression. They have abused their position of power as employers, exploiting the poor by withholding the wages of laborers (see Deut. 24:14–15). Day laborers depended completely on their meager pay. To withhold their wages was to attack their very lives—it was in fact gradually to kill them, an accusation that is made directly in 5:6. For this reason, James strikingly depicts wages as the very blood of the workers crying out in protest against injustice and declares that these cries, along with the cries of the exploited laborers themselves, "have reached the ears of the Lord of hosts."

Second, James censures the rich for their pampered lives: "You have lived on the earth in luxury and in pleasure." The hardship they have inflicted on others stands in sharp contrast to the softness of their own living. James explicitly notes that they lived *on the earth* in a self-indulgent manner—a state that will not last forever.

IS JAMES ADDRESSING
RICH CHRISTIANS?

Is James attacking wealthy members of the Christian community? Interpreters tend to agree that James is probably not attacking Christians! It is doubtful that "the rich people" censured were actually Christians, for in the three passages in which "the rich" are mentioned (1:9–11; 2:6–7; 5:1–6), they appear to be regarded as "outsiders"—people who are not members of the Christian community. There is no attempt to influence the rich. The condemnation is absolute. There is no call to repentance.

More than likely, the Christian communities with which the author was most closely associated were largely from the lower end of the economic spectrum. There were some people of means within these congregations. Small merchants, for example, appear to be addressed in 4:13–17 (though they are not designated as "the rich"). Moreover, rich visitors were beginning to frequent worship services (2:1–13)—indeed they were being fawned over, and the author feared this development.

Most of the people whom James first addressed, however, were poor. Interpreters suspect that James's harsh words of condemnation in 5:1–6 aim to give comfort and consolation to those who had experienced real hardship at the hands of the rich. They are also words of warning about the danger of riches.

As professor of preaching Tom Long imagines,

> Brother James is, in effect, preaching an epistolary sermon to a congregation of Christians who are, among other things, on the low side economically. At one dramatic point in the sermon (5:1), James strides away from the pulpit, flings open a window of the little sanctuary and begins to shout toward the Manor House, "Come now, you rich, weep and howl. . . . Your gold and silver have rusted. . . ." The congregation watches and listens in stunned silence as their pastor shouts dire warnings toward the rich, toward the powerful, toward the folks who control the society. "Behold," thunders James, "the wages of the laborers who mowed your fields, which you kept back by fraud, cry out. . . ." Now the congregation begins to get into the sermon. An "amen" from a laborer in the back pew is heard, then another "amen" and another, until the tiny church is filled with a chorus of amens. ("The Use of Scripture," 351)

In other words, the harsh words of condemnation in 5:1–6 are "good news" to the people whom James first addressed. For what James announces is that there will come a day when the poor will be lifted up and when the rich will be held accountable for injustice. These words continue to be good news to the poor of this world to this day.

North American Christian congregations, however, are wealthy when measured by international standards. Is James's angry tirade relevant to our lives? Absolutely! It continues to serve as a warning of the dangers of riches. Do not James's words also call us to repentance—"to work and pray for the day when we will not wear anything or eat anything or use anything that is wet in God's sight with human tears, or cheapened by wearing down the lives of the weak" (Rauschenbush, *Prayers*, 65–66)?

Moreover, this passage reminds us that God wills justice for the poor and that God hears the cries of the oppressed. And if this is so, are we not called to redress the crippling inequities and injustices with which many of our brothers and sisters must daily contend? As James so forcefully reminds us, "faith by itself, if it has no works, is dead" (2:17).

18. Final Words of Counsel
for the Christian Community
James 5:7–20

One of the fastest growing religious constituencies today is that of "believers, but not belongers"—persons who say they hold to religious beliefs but who choose not to participate in a local congregation or to identify themselves with the community of faith through the ages. But to James's way of thinking, there is no such thing as a private Christian. To be a Christian is to be part of a community of faith. Thus the closing words of the letter seek to strengthen the faithful in their common life. James's counsel is threefold: The community is to wait patiently for the coming of the Lord; it is to be united in prayer; and its members are to demonstrate care and concern for one another.

THE FUTURE HORIZON
James 5:7–11

> 5:7 **Be patient, therefore, beloved, until the coming of the Lord. The farmer waits for the precious crop from the earth, being patient with it until it receives the early and the late rains.** 8 **You also most be patient. Strengthen your hearts, for the coming of the Lord is near.** 9 **Beloved, do not grumble against one another, so that you may not be judged. See, the Judge is standing at the doors!** 10 **As an example of suffering and patience, beloved, take the prophets who spoke in the name of the Lord.** 11 **Indeed we call blessed those who showed endurance. You have heard of the endurance of Job, and you have seen the purpose of the Lord, how the Lord is compassionate and merciful.**

James lifted our eyes to the future horizon in 5:1–6 and now continues to speak of the last days, but introduces another element. The angry threats subside, and the tone changes dramatically as James encourages the Christian community: "Be patient, therefore, beloved, until the coming of the Lord."

Many of James's first readers were in much need of encouragement. Some experienced hardship at the hands of the rich (see 2:6–7; 5:1–6). Whatever the nature of their difficulties, or of ours, believers are encouraged to be patient in view of the imminent coming of the Lord. A model of fortitude is provided: the farmer who "waits for the precious crop from the earth, being patient with it until it receives the early and the late rains."

In addition, James commends two examples of patience under hardship: The Old Testament prophets, whose struggles against opposition and rejection and temptations to despair (see Jer. 20:7–9) were well known; and the proverbially patient Job, an example likely to surprise those who are familiar with the defiant Job of the canonical book. In chapters 3—31 of the Old Testament book, Job agonizes over his predicament and struggles loudly and bitterly with his pain before well-meaning friends and the Almighty. Nevertheless, he clings tenaciously to God and refuses to yield to atheism. Thus patience or "endurance" is not equated with passive resignation. What James recommends is active perseverance—a steadfast, heroic constancy of faith. Those who know the outcome of Job's story ("the purpose of the Lord" [James 5:11]; compare Job 42:12) can be confident that their hope, too, is in this "compassionate and merciful" God.

To be sure, the author of James believed that Christ would return during his lifetime, as did other first-century Christians (see 1 Thess. 4:14–17). We no longer live with the same sense of *imminent* expectation. Nevertheless, hope in Christ's coming again is still an essential article of Christian faith. We are to wait patiently and to live in hope, assured that whatever difficulties beset us, the ultimate fact for the world will be the power and love of God.

God has a gracious, saving purpose for the world—a purpose seen clearly in Jesus Christ. And God will not fail to achieve that redemptive purpose in the world despite all appearances to the contrary. Christ will come again, and God's reign will be established in fullness: "a new heaven and a new earth" (Rev. 21:1). To that end we pray, "Your kingdom come, your will be done on earth as it is in heaven." Thus we too can move into the future with patient trust and confidence, knowing that the future belongs to God.

THE IMPORTANCE OF PRAYER
James 5:12–18

> 5:12 **Above all, my beloved, do not swear, either by heaven or by earth or by any other oath, but let your "Yes" be yes and your "No" be no, so that you may not fall under condemnation.**

 [13] **Are any among you suffering? They should pray. Are any cheerful? They should sing songs of praise. [14] Are any among you sick? They should call for the elders of the church and have them pray over them, anointing them with oil in the name of the Lord. [15] The prayer of faith will save the sick, and the Lord will raise them up; and anyone who has committed sins will be forgiven. [16] Therefore confess your sins to one another, and pray for one another, so that you may be healed. The prayer of the righteous is powerful and effective. [17] Elijah was a human being like us, and he prayed fervently that it might not rain, and for three years and six months it did not rain on the earth. [18] Then he prayed again, and the heaven gave rain and the earth yielded its harvest.**

The Christian community is also to be united in prayer, which is a vital aspect of the community's life. Earlier, James has indicated that there are inappropriate ways of calling upon God (1:6; 4:3), and one more is noted: that of swearing "by heaven or by earth or by any other oath."

James is not speaking here of profanity, or of the oaths required in legal or civil proceedings. What James condemns is the practice of appealing to God or to something sacred in order to buttress the truthfulness of a statement or promise. Swearing by oath is unnecessary for Christians, who should always be honest and sincere in relations with others. A simple yes or no should suffice (see Matthew 5:33–37).

This letter also addresses the appropriate forms of prayer.

1. We are to pray when we are suffering—that God may strengthen us, direct us, and give us assurance to press on.
2. We are to pray when we are cheerful—in thanksgiving for the grace of God, which blesses us with experiences of fullness.
3. We are to pray when we are sick—calling upon the healing power of God, who wills our restoration and wholeness.

All the circumstances of our lives are then occasions of prayer!

Moreover, prayer is not only personal, it is also communal. Believers are encouraged to join the power of personal prayer with the prayer of others. The sick are instructed to "call for the elders of the church and have them pray over them, anointing them with oil in the name of the Lord." The "elders," it seems, took special responsibility for the physical as well as spiritual good of the congregation. Thus they would gather to pray for and with the sick and to anoint them with oil. In the ancient world, oil had both a medicinal and a liturgical purpose. James makes it clear that it is not the oil but the power of God in response to faithful prayer that brings healing from sickness (5:15).

James also affirms that if the sick person has committed a sin, he or she will be forgiven. A direct connection between sickness and sin is not necessarily assumed, but a possible connection may be implied. Whatever one may think of this ancient view, Christians today affirm that God wills restoration to both physical and spiritual wholeness.

This latter aspect of human wholeness is directly addressed in 5:16. James acknowledges the reality of sin. It remains a fact of Christian life. The proper response to it is prayer. Believers are encouraged to confess their sins to one another and to pray for one another, so that they may be restored to wholeness of life. The prayer of all believing petitioners is powerful and effective. Great results can be expected through prayer.

Lest there be any doubt about this, James points to the prophet Elijah to demonstrate how effective and powerful prayer can be. James emphasizes Elijah's energy in prayer ("he prayed fervently") and his humanity. The one who prayed with such great effect was an ordinary "human being like us." By this example, James encourages Christians to place great confidence in prayer.

CARE AND CONCERN
FOR ONE ANOTHER
James 5:19–20

> 5:19 **My brothers and sisters, if anyone among you wanders from the truth and is brought back by another, ²⁰ you should know that whoever brings back a sinner from wandering will save the sinner's soul from death and will cover a multitude of sins.**

In closing, James encourages members of the Christian community to have greater care and concern for one another. Sin is a fact of life, and Christians do wander away at times "from the truth" and from the community. James focuses not on the person who sins, but on the responsibility incumbent upon other Christians to seek actively to restore the sinner.

Christians are not to give up on each other! We have a responsibility for brothers and sisters in Christ who wander from our fellowship. We are to seek to win them back and preserve them from error. When confronted with human sin, our attitude is always to be one of restoration rather than condemnation. James points out that attempts to win back a brother or sister who has gone astray are well worth the effort, for "whoever brings back a sinner from wandering will save the sinner's soul from death and will cover a multitude of sins." James's final word is this assurance of blessing.

Works Cited

Hebrews

Attridge, Harold W. *The Epistle to the Hebrews*. Hermeneia. Philadelphia: Fortress Press, 1989.

Chilstrom, Herbert W. *Hebrews: A New and Better Way*. Philadelphia: Fortress Press, 1984.

Hagner, Donald A. *Hebrews*. New International Biblical Commentary. Peabody, Mass.: Hendrickson Publishers, 1990.

Isaacs, Marie E. *Sacred Space: An Approach to the Theology of the Epistle to the Hebrews*. Journal for the Study of the New Testament Supplement Series, 83. Sheffield: JSOT Press, 1992.

Johnsson, William G. *Hebrews*. Knox Preaching Guides. Atlanta: John Knox Press, 1980.

Lewis, C. S. *The Screwtape Letters*. New York: The MacMillan Company, 1943.

The hymn "Draw Near and Take the Body of the Lord" is translated by John M. Neale, 1818, and is found in the *Lutheran Book of Worship*, 226. Minneapolis: Augsburg Fortress, 1978.

James

Buechner, Frederick. *Telling the Truth: The Gospel as Tragedy, Comedy, and Fairy Tale*. San Francisco: HarperSanFrancisco, 1977.

Campbell, Ernest. "Toward a Protestant Doctrine of Works." National Radio Pulpit. New York: Broadcasting and Film Communications, NCCCUSA, 1974. Audiocassette.

Felder, Cain Hope. *Troubling Biblical Waters: Race, Class and Family*. Maryknoll, N.Y.: Orbis Books, 1989.

Johnson, Luke T. "Friendship with the World/Friendship with God: A Study of Discipleship in James," in *Discipleship in the New Testament,* ed. F. F. Segovia, 166–83. Philadelphia: Fortress Press, 1985.

Jones, Peter Rhea. "Approaches to the Study of James," in *Review and Expositor* 66 (1969):426.

King, Martin Luther, Jr. *Stride Toward Freedom: The Montgomery Story.* New York: Harper & Brothers, 1958.

Laws, Sophie. *A Commentary on the Epistle of James.* Harper's New Testament Commentaries. San Francisco: Harper & Row, 1980.

Long, Tom. "The Use of Scripture in Contemporary Preaching," in *Interpretation* 44 (1990):351.

Rauschenbush, Walter. *Prayers of the Social Awakening.* Boston: Pilgrim Press, 1925.

Review and Expositor 83 (1986):355–438. Whole issue on James.

Tamez, Elsa. *The Scandalous Message of James: Faith Without Works is Dead.* New York: Crossroad, 1990.